Indian Warfare in Western Pennsylvania and North West Virginia at the Time of the American Revolution

Including
the Narrative of Indian and Tory Depradations
by John Crawford,
the Military Reminiscences of Captain Henry Jolly,
and
The Narrative of Lydia Boggs Shepherd Cruger

Edited by Jared C. Lobdell
with Notes by Lyman Copeland Draper

Published for the Draper Society

HERITAGE BOOKS, INC.

From the author of:

*Recollections of Lewis Bonnett Jr. (1778-1850)
And the Bonnett and Wetzel Families*

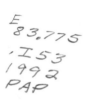

Published 1992 By

Heritage Books, Inc.
1540-E Pointer Ridge Place
Bowie, Maryland 20716
(301) 390-7709

ISBN 1-55613-653-6

A Complete Catalog Listing Hundreds Of Titles On
Genealogy, History, And Americana
Available Free On Request

Table of Contents

APPENDIX I:

APPENDIX II:

APPENDIX III:

APPENDIX IV:

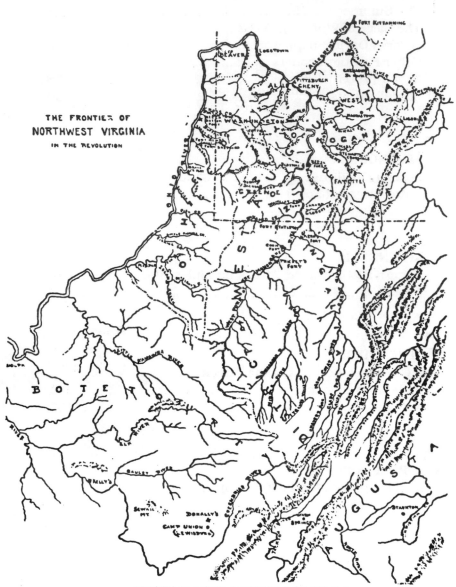

THE FRONTIER OF
NORTHWEST VIRGINIA
IN THE REVOLUTION

Adapted (and very considerably expanded westward) from sketch map in
Boyd Crumrine, Washington County, Pa. (Philadelphia, 1882)

Introduction

THIS BOOK IS part -- I hope -- of the fulfillment of a dream, not only of mine but of one of the greatest neglected men of the nineteenth century. That man was Lyman Copeland Draper, from 1854 to 1886 the Secretary of the Wisconsin Historical Society (now the State Historical Society of Wisconsin). Both before and after those years he was the indefatigable collector of reminiscences (he was among our first oral historians) and original documents relating to the heroic age of American expansion westward, from the years before the American Revolution to the end of the War of 1812. From his early years in the field, travelling tens of thousands of miles by horseback, interviewing survivors of that great push westward, Draper dreamt of a series of books presenting the heroism of these pioneers, and presenting it (so far as we can judge from what he published) as much as possible in their own words.

The result of his endeavors is to be found in the nearly 500 manuscript volumes in the Draper Collection of the State Historical Society of Wisconsin at Madison, in the texts he edited for the first ten volumes of the *Wisconsin Historical Collections*, in the papers he published in these *Collections* and elsewhere, in his magisterial work on *King's Mountain and Its Heroes* (1881), and not least in the five volumes edited by Reuben Gold Thwaites and Louise Phelps Kellogg, beginning with *A Documentary History of Dunmore's War* (Madison: 1905, reprinted Bowie, MD: Heritage Books Inc., 1989) and ending (incompletely) with *Frontier Retreat on the Upper Ohio* (Madison: 1917). The final volume of the series, covering the years 1781-1783 was never published -- indeed, so far as I know, it was not prepared for publication.

A small group of Draper's admirers have now formed the Draper Society, to take up where he left off at his death a century ago, and this book is among the first fruits of our work. The very first fruits were in my edition of *Recollections of Lewis Bonnett, Jr. (1778-1850) and the Bonnett and Wetzel Families* (Bowie, MD: Heritage Books Inc., 1991). I have only with the greatest reluctance limited this publication to the three items it contains, with some relevant appendices -- but I have done so knowing how our society's namesake fell into the habit of seeking perfection before publication, and thus failing to publish. There are at least three other memoirs or reminiscences that could well have been published in this volume, and indeed Captain Jolly and Mrs. Cruger could have accompanied Major Bonnett last year. But these accounts have waited a century and a half, and they can wait a year or two longer. The other accounts, by the way, are an account of the Captivity of the Henry Children by one of them, the memoirs of Stephen Burkam (though these have been published in part in an account of William Crawford's Sandusky Campaign in the *Western Pennsylvania Historical Magazine*), and George Edgington's Memoirs. These will, I trust, appear in a subsequent Draper society volume.

ABOUT THE AUTHORS

John Crawford compiled his family chronicle of events in Western Pennsylvania from the stories of his relatives: he is a chronicler of the events he recounts, but not a participant in them, at least until 1777, when he is a five-year-old child, hauled half-asleep on horseback to the safety of a neighboring fort. Still, his is the best -- in many cases the only -- story we have of these events. The narrators whose memoirs and reminiscences make up the remainder of this volume (less three of the appendices) were participants. They are Captain Henry Jolly (1757-1842) and Mrs. Lydia Boggs Shepherd Cruger (1766-1867).

Captain Jolly is the representative here of the generation who were frontier soldiers on the Upper Ohio at the time of the Revolution, and he was the only such soldier who, having carried on as a frontier scout after the war, left an account of his military career, unless one counts the unfortunate General Richard Butler (1749-1791) and his brothers. Not all of Captain Jolly's reminiscences deal with the frontier, inasmuch as he was one of Morgan's Rifle Regiment in the Jerseys and at Saratoga and around Philadelphia in 1777.

Mrs. Cruger was a girl of sixteen at the time of the third and final Indian/British siege of Fort Henry (Wheeling) in 1782, and this portion of her narrative covers events she herself witnessed -- as does much of her narrative for 1781. But she married Moses Shepherd, son of Colonel David Shepherd, who commanded at Fort Henry in 1777, and is recognized as a respectable source of information for that siege also. Nevertheless, it is principally to the third siege of Fort Henry (1782) that her narrative is devoted.

ABOUT THE GEOGRAPHY OF THE AREA

The premier geographer of the Upper Ohio was William Darby (1775-1854), who will be recalled from the Bonnett volume, and who resided for a brief time as a schoolteacher in Wheeling (then Virginia), in the house of Henry Jolly, shortly before Jolly moved to the Northwest Territory. We have met him in the Bonnett Recollections and we will have occasion to meet him yet again in subsequent Draper Society publications. His letters to Lyman Draper, published in the late lamented *Western Pennsylvania Historical Magazine*, include some further references to Henry Jolly. Let us for the moment emulate Darby in examining the geography of this frontier, and the effect of that geography on its history, so that Jolly's reminiscences and the others can be placed in context. Those readers who have already examined the *Recollections of Lewis Bonnett, Jr.*, the first volume published by the Draper Society, will (I hope) forgive me if much of what follows appears also in the introduction to that volume. The facts of geography, after all, do not change from one Draper volume to the next, and Captain Jolly and Mrs. Cruger lived not far from the Bonnett and Wetzel households.

The Allegheny River, flowing from the north, and the Monongahela from the south, join at the Forks of the Ohio (present Point State Park) in Pittsburgh, once Fort King George, then Fort Duquesne, and then Fort Pitt. In 1755, British Major-General Edward Braddock built a road from Alexandria, Virginia, almost to the Forks of the Ohio, before he was stopped and killed and his men routed in present-day Braddock, Pennsylvania, just southeast of Pittsburgh, along the mainline of what used to be the Pennsylvania Railroad. Three years later, in 1758, British Major-General John Forbes built a road over the mountains from Carlisle, Pennsylvania, reaching the Forks of the Ohio, and driving the French out of Fort Duquesne, which he renamed Fort Pitt before he died of a fever a few months later. He had with him a young Virginia Colonel named George Washington.

The Forbes road made the country around and beyond Pittsburgh (Fort Pitt) accessible to eastern Pennsylvania, and thus to New Jersey and New York City. The Braddock road made it accessible to Virginia and western Maryland. But though the country was accessible, there is a question whether its settlement was legal under the Quebec Act and the Great Proclamation. Though this matter is dealt with in our first volume, it should also perhaps be dealt with here.

In a practical sense, the end of the French and Indian War in 1763 and the passing of control from the French to the English in the valley of the Ohio opened the way for settlement between the mountains and the Ohio. But the Royal Proclamation of October 7, 1763, forbade settlement by European Americans on "any lands beyond the heads or sources of any of the rivers which fall into the Atlantic Ocean from the west or northwest" (quoted in D. W. Meinig, *Atlantic America 1492-1800*, p. 284).

This restriction, as Professor Meinig remarks, left the lands on the Cherokee frontier to the southward (what is now Tennessee and the Carolinas on south) in Cherokee hands -- indeed, the Europeans had not reached the sources or headwaters of the rivers in question there, though they soon reached the Holston, and the war on the Cherokee frontier began by 1776.

Also, the restriction left the lands on the Iroquois frontier to the northward (west of the Mohawk Country) in Iroquois hands, for what was true of the Europeans in the south was true of the Europeans in the north -- they had not yet reached the headwaters of the westward-flowing rivers. The first one they reached was the Allegheny, later in the 1760s.

But in the center, there had been settlement coming up the Potomac and Juniata to the Monongahela and Youghiogheny, as well as up the Shenandoah to the New River, to the Kanawha (Kenhawa) and the Ohio or the Holston (and then the Tennessee). At the time of the Great Proclamation, several thousand settlers were west of the line separated the headwaters of headwaters of Atlantic rivers from the Mississippi River basin.

By 1771, cessions and adjustments had moved the Proclamation Line to the Ohio River running from the Great Forks at Pittsburgh to the mouth of the Kentucky. And the Quebec Act of 1774 established that boundary by law.

In this connection, it is important that the Ohio River flows northward from the Forks to the mouth of Beaver Creek, before turning southwestward toward present-day Parkersburg, West Virginia. The Monongahela country, southwestern Pennsylvania and the Northern Panhandle of what is now West Virginia, were thus not beyond the Ohio and were open to settlement by the colonists (admittedly, many of them already settled there), to whom the Ohio Country proper was (theoretically) banned.

Of course, what happened in Philadelphia on July 4th, 1776, changed things, leading eventually to the Northwest Ordinance of 1787, and then far beyond. But the course of westward expansion between 1763 and 1776 was essentially determined by three factors, at least in this middle part of the frontier: the laying out of Braddock's road, the laying out of the Forbes road, and the way the Ohio flowed from the Great Forks. The location of the settlements, in addition, depended on the location of creeks and branches of fresh water, and the records and reminiscences of these years chronicle events on the three forks of Wheeling Creek and on Dunkard's, Graves, Tenmile and Buffalo Creeks, all of them flowing into the Monongahela or the Ohio.

It is on these creeks flowing into the Monogahela that the events of Crawford's Narrative take place, but on the Upper Ohio proper that the events take place recounted by Captain Jolly and Mrs. Cruger. The exceptions are the carrying of captives to Quebec (the present Quebec City) or Detroit, which was the seat of British military operations in the Old Northwest during the War of the Revolution, and the campaign against the Christian Indians (converted by the Moravian missionaries and thus known as Moravians) in east central Ohio, along what is now I-77.

Not all the traffic overland followed the military roads: there were still some travellers who took the old Indian trails, and beyond Fort Pitt there were no roads until 1795 or 1796, when Zane's Trace was laid out from Wheeling to present-day Zanesville, Ohio, and thence south to Maysville, Kentucky. Traffic from Pittsburgh to Wheeling was mostly river traffic. Braddock had followed an Indian trail from Cumberland, Maryland, to the environs in which he was attacked and killed -- or, to be strictly accurate, he had followed Nemacolin's Trail, which had been partially improved by George Washington and Thomas Cresap, among others, in the years from 1750 to 1754. Another trail, or perhaps a branch of the same trail, led from Braddock's road to the mouth of Redstone Creek, and another, skirting Redstone, through Catfish Camp (now Washington, Pennsylvania), led to the Mouth of Wheeling (at present-day Wheeling, West Virginia). The Redstone trail is sometimes called Burd's road, after the militia officer who improved it in 1759, but it was not a proper military road like Braddock's or the Forbes road. There was also an improved trail, sometimes called Dunlap's Road, up from Winchester, Virginia, to the Fort Pitt country.

The Upper Ohio -- that is, the area bounded by the Ohio River from the Forks (Pittsburgh) to its turn westward along what is now the southern boundary of the State of Ohio, and including the Monongahela watershed and the tributaries of the Ohio south and east of the river -- was the midpoint of the American frontier from 1763 into the 1790s, besides being (in a sense) its spearpoint beyond the Atlantic watershed.

Other frontiers have their stories in the manuscripts in Lyman Draper's collection. For now, our story lies principally in the area that Virginia called the District of West Augusta, and which Pennsylvania now calls Washington and Fayette counties (with excursions into Greene and Allegheny and even Beaver and Westmoreland), and West Virginia calls Ohio County. Some of this Pennsylvania area, Washington County in particular, was not only settled in part from Virginia (and Maryland), but until 1780 was claimed by Virginia as Yohogania County in the District of West Augusta.

There were Indian depredations -- attacks and solitary scalpings, frontier muggings, so to speak, in a seemingly endless turf battle -- well before the British stirred up the Indians after the War of the American Revolution began. There were expeditions beyond the Ohio, as far as the Muskingum, while the settlers were still British subjects -- at least, there was one in 1774 (and the best account of it may still be in an unpublished book by Lyman Draper) -- and there was "Dunmore's" War, in which the Royal Governor of Virginia, John Murray, fourth Earl of Dunmore, reluctantly came to battle with the Indians because he could not prevent his backwoodsmen from coming up from Virginia to attack the tribes at Point Pleasant (now in West Virginia). There was an engagement between the settlers and the Indians in the Valley of Virginia as early as 1742 (Draper wrote an unpublished account of it, which we hope soon to publish, with supporting documents), and throughout the 1750s and 1760s there was a constant and bloody jostling of White and Indian along this frontier.

But these were expeditions and skirmishes and even battles in which the forces came from the east and at a time when the settlers mostly looked to the east for help. Then, at almost a single point in time, a point about where Captain Henry Jolly's memoirs begin, there came a change: the settlers stopped looking toward the east and the government to defend them, and started planning and carrying out the struggle on their own. They even sometimes went back over the mountains to the defense of the east.

Perhaps the change began when the government abandoned Fort Pitt in 1772. Perhaps it was almost full-blown when Colonel Andrew Lewis won Lord Dunmore's War for him in 1774. Whatever the time and the origin, the attitude is characteristic of the entire Heroic Age on the Upper Ohio. This change is, by the way, a theme of Dale Van Every's quartet of volumes on the frontier, and particularly *Forth to the Wilderness* (New York: 1961).

The cabins were occupied in the winters, which can be long and cold on the western slopes of the Alleghanies, and in the summer, when the Indians were out and about, the settlers "forted" in some central stockade built around the cabin of one of the larger-familied settlers. One of these, in our area -- Rice's Fort on the Dutch Fork of the Buffalo -- was the scene of what may well have been the last land engagement of the War of the American Revolution, at the end of the Indian season of 1782. The appendices to this book print accounts of the war on Dutch Fork the previous year, in connection with the Jolly and Cruger Narratives of the 1781 campaign.

When they forted during the Indian season, the settlers still worked their own fields, and of course would rather have been in their own homes than in the fort. But it was while they were at home, or while they were working the fields, that they were most likely to be attacked: the history of the time is a history of the pull between the (relative) safety of the fort and the desirability of being in one's home on one's own land. All too often, the land (and with it the Indian tomahawk) won out.

JOHN CRAWFORD'S NARRATIVE

The Narrative is found in Draper MSS 6NN:77-102, and was left incomplete at its author's death in 1831, before he reached the period for which he would have been an eye witness (barring two events he remembers from the age of five, in 1777). It deals with a slightly different part of the frontier from Jolly's and Mrs. Cruger's (though it touches hers when she recounts the first siege of Wheeling in 1777), and it deals mostly with a slightly earlier period, but it provides a good background for understanding the frontier *milieu*. It is also an important account of the pivotal year of 1777 on the Monogahela. In its early portions, it reminds me of nothing so much as the family chronicles that make up so much of the historical literature of sixteenth-century Scotland, and it is, in a sense, their direct descendant.

As noted, it was left unfinished at the author's death in 1831, and so far as we can tell, it was written as a continuous document in that year, not long before his death. Although it is recorded in the Draper MSS as covering the years 1770-1777, it is in fact divided pretty much into two parts, the first covering the years up to 1777 (with much of it before 1770), concentrating on the history of the author's particular branch of the Crawford family. The second part covers the events of 1777 along the lower (northern) portion of the Monongahela, as remembered by John Crawford (who was five in that year) and as told him by his father William Crawford (b. 1744). This William Crawford is not to be confused with the Colonel William Crawford (1730-1782) who lost his life in the Sandusky massacre, being there burned at the stake by the victorious "Indian" forces. (Those who have read my introduction to the *Recollections of Lewis Bonnett, Jr.* will understand the quotation marks.) The Sandusky massacre was the response to the murder of the Moravian Indians by Washington County militia under Colonel David Williamson (1753-1809) the year before.

Other than the brief note in Josephine Draper's *Guide* to the Draper MSS (Madison: 1983), I know of only one reference to the Crawford Narrative. In Thwaites and Kellogg, *Frontier Defense on the Upper Ohio* (Madison: 1912), p. 143, the MS is said to deal with the death of the Tory, Hickson or Higgison, on the Cheat River: the reference is to 6NN: 86-101. But, though Hickson is mentioned briefly on p. 101 of Draper MS 6NN (in a comparison with the violence of the backcountry conflict in North Carolina), there is no other mention of this case anywhere in the text. There is a Tory T. H. mentioned earlier, but this is not Hickson (or Higgison). It may well be a Thomas Hughes (there were two), listed in Springhill Township in 1772 (Veech, *The Monongahela of Old.* Reprinted Waynesburg, PA: 1971, p. 201).

One particular attraction of the Crawford Narrative is the occasional interjection of the author's own memories (being bundled on to a horse and falling off, asleep, in the creek, on the occasion of a false alarm that sent his family to take refuge in a fort), although the Narrative is in general based on what he has been told by his father. At perhaps too great length, he draws parallels between the Federalists of the War of 1812 and the Tories of 1777, to the advantage of the latter, though they were (in his view) ignorant and treacherous. I have left these in the text because they bring the author alive: he is a Jeffersonian -- he will not even permit the Federalists the use of their name because they seek to undermine the Federal Government. The innkeeper at Pittsburgh who would prefer to be ruled by Great Britain than by the mob is, he assures us, the "only black sheep" of his family.

The year 1777 was important in the lands along the Monongahela and the Ohio. It was the year in which Simon Girty and Alexander McKee finally cast their lot with the Tories, and indeed the first year in which Whig and Tory were names really applicable along the frontier where only three years before the British Royal Governor of Virginia and Colonel Andrew Lewis (whom Washington suggested as commander-in-chief in 1775) had joined in fighting the Battle of Point Pleasant and Lord Dunmore's War. The Crawford Narrative gives us a small-scale snapshot of what was happening more widely. The focus is on the Monongahela from what is now the West Virginia line to Redstone (Brownsville, Pennsylvania). We learn of several forts of whose existence I was previously ignorant. Miner's fort on Whitely Creek is one; Provence's, I thought initially, was another. Even the spelling of the latter seems to be unsure. In the list of settlers in Veech (pp. 201-202) it is Provance (in Springhill Township), while in the muster roll of Captain John Wetzel's company of Rangers, Monongalia County (of which our William Crawford was a lieutenant) it is Province (*Frontier Defense*, p. 305). In Crawford's Narrative it is uniformly Provence. The fort is not located on either the map in *Frontier Defense* or the map in Boyd Crumrine's *History of Washington County, PA* (Philadelphia: 1882), which is reprinted in this volume on page VI and which does include Miner's fort.

I said I thought initially that I was unfamiliar with Provance's fort, but as I was writing this introduction, some dim recollection led me to Allan Eckert's *The Frontiersmen* (Boston: 1967), which is woven around the life of Simon Kenton (1755-1836). Evidently relying on the *Journal of William Grills* (Baltimore: 1808), Eckert recounts young Simon Kenton's first association (1771) with Jacob Greathouse and Grills, at Provance's settlement, which Eckert locates just west of present Masontown, Pennsylvania, on Big Whitely Creek (*passim*, Chapter I and note, p. 592).

Draper obtained the MS of the Crawford Narrative from John Crawford's son, John Lynn Crawford. I suppose it was written in response to Alexander Scott Withers' *Chronicles of Border Warfare*, which had appeared earlier in 1831, from the press of Joseph Israel in Clarksburg, and which concentrates on the area of North West Virginia more than on Southwestern Pennsylvania. Even Joseph Doddridge, who grew up in the same area as John Crawford (and was three years older), covered very little of the year of 1777 in his *Notes* (Wellsburg: 1824).

The map included here from Crumrine's *History* can be used as a guide to Crawford's Narrative, as well as the others in this volume -- but it is the eastern part of the map for his and the western part for Captain Jolly's and Mrs. Cruger's.

So far as I know, Crawford's account of Hickson's death is the only one referring to the possible drunkenness of the "Whig party" in the canoe. His account of oathtaking, and of the intermixture of Whig and Tory in the forts, is unique in my experience of frontier memoirs -- though, to be sure, it is his father talking and not he. And occasionally we are brought up short -- as when Margaret McDowell (the midwife) is the "only physician" in the country, and prescribes anointment with black cat's blood as a cure for the shingles. (But Crawford suggests that a white cat's blood would presumably have been equally efficacious: the world of 1831 is measurably closer to us than the world of 1777.)

Lyman Draper filled in some of the names for which Crawford gave only initials. I have filled in a few others. Except for these, the square brackets in the text generally represent words I have added to make sense of the text -- words that I believe Crawford inadvertently omitted. Some words he omitted he has added with carets pointing to them, but he did not finish his task.

John Crawford was a lifelong resident of what is now Greene County, Pennsylvania, near the Fayette County line. His career as an expert on waterways and a stalwart of the Democratic Republican Party (Jeffersonians) is not relevant to this Narrative, except for the story of his visit to Pittsburgh in 1814, for the purposes of the first and giving rise to reflections on the second. Unlike Jolly he is not recollecting his own military career, and unlike Mrs. Cruger he is not relying on his own experience or the experiences of men and women of his generation. He speaks to us alternately in his voice and his father's. But he tells a little-told story pretty well, and the reader can go from his account of the Tory affairs of 1777 to Mrs. Cruger's account of the First Siege of Wheeling, and acquire a pretty fair idea of what was going on in that year, far from Captain Jolly's experiences at Saratoga.

THE REMINISCENCES OF HENRY JOLLY

The author of these reminiscences, Captain Henry Jolly, was born in Chester County, Pennsylvania, December 20, 1757, as his recollections tell us. He died in Licking County, Ohio, on July 29, 1842, having given his name to a township in Washington County, Ohio, and having served as a Judge in his adopted state, to which he had moved in the 1790s, when it was still the Territory Northwest of the River Ohio. He was eulogized in the *National Intelligencer* by the frontier geographer William Darby as "the last remnant of our heroic age." Darby continued in these words:

"It is not injustice to him to say he was inferior to Lewis Wetzel, Jonathan Zane, Frank McGuire, and perhaps some few others" in his "knowledge of the wilds on both sides of the Ohio" but "as his education was altogether superior to any of the persons named, and his regular service under [Daniel] Morgan had given him ideas and habits of caution and discipline, in which qualities the early pioneer warriors were generally most deplorably deficient, the return of Jolly to the western frontier [in 1779] (...) and his services there were inexpressibly valuable. Few hearts are now left to beat with gratitude who were sixty years ago made glad when they knew that Henry Jolly stood between them and danger. Of these few I am one."

It is, perhaps, ironic, that (this being among the first of the Draper Society publications) the letters incorporating Henry Jolly's reminiscences were written not to Lyman Copeland Draper, but to that earlier historian of the Ohio Valley, Samuel P. Hildreth. They are contained in Draper MSS 6 NN, a collection of papers gathered by Hildreth and other antiquaries (including Joseph Doddridge and Robert Orr, Jr.) in their own earlier research on the border wars.

The letters were written between 1831 and 1838, and their proper bibliographic description is Draper 6 NN: 28-61, with sheet no. 28 including 28/1 through 28/4 and covering Captain Jolly's experience in the east as one of Morgan's riflemen. Earlier in this century, the pagination began at p. 24 (as can be seen in Thwaites and Kellogg *Frontier Advance on the Upper Ohio* (Madison: 1916), pp. 184, 211, 257. The quarto sheet breaks off in the middle of a sentence, to which I have supplied a conclusion from his review of Withers and from other sources.

The rank of Captain dates, as we eventually discover in Jolly's text, from a commission signed by the Governor of Virginia on the 1st of July, 1790 (Draper MSS 6NN:50). He was originally commissioned Ensign in the Company of Captain Lewis Bonnett, Sr., in the Spring of 1784, and on Bonnett's resignation shortly thereafter (or perhaps in 1786) was commissioned Captain, and then re-commissioned after the adoption of the U. S. Constitution in 1789. These were Militia commissions, but the militia was called into Federal service, and in any case (given the lack of an army in the period 1784-1789), Captain Jolly may surely be considered to have spent eighteen years (1776-1794) in the military service of his country, though neither he nor any of his colleagues even in the Federalized Militia are listed in Heitman, *Historical Register and Dictionary of the United States Army* (Washington: 1903). I believe they should be, at least for their service in President Washington's Indian War (1790-1794), if not perhaps under the Articles of Confederation.

After his retirement from active military service in 1794, Captain Jolly moved to what is now Ohio, and there, as a Democratic Republican (Jeffersonian), served as a Judge in Union County for seven years, as a County Commissioner, and as a member of the Ohio Legislature. In 1838 Samuel Hildreth, anticipating Draper, corresponded with him, seeking information on the Ohio Frontier ("Ohio" meaning, in this context, the River Ohio). The letters from which these reminiscences are taken are the result of Hildreth's inquiries. They were eventually acquired by Lyman Copeland Draper and are to be found, as we have noted, in the State Historical Society of Wisconsin (Madison, Wisconsin) in Draper MSS 6NN.

In a few of the letters, Jolly comments on other matters of interest to him, if not to Dr. Hildreth. In the letter of January 3, 1838 (6NN:44), he writes "I also will tell you about cutworms, budworms, grassworms, catterpillars, deers, bears, etc., etc. A buffaloe I never seen in the State of Ohio. Elks I haven't seen in Ohio." I assume that the "in Ohio" is in contradistinction to an unstated (West) Virginia or Pennsylvania, where in his time there were both buffalo and elk.

From time to time, Jolly comments on other informants and other accounts of the war on the borders (in particular). He also provides a review of Alexander Withers, *Chronicles of Border Warfare* (Clarksburg, Virginia: 1831). I have placed this as an appendix to his reminiscences, which it occasionally repeats. Otherwise, the comments on other matters in the letters form part of the text of his reminiscences. Both Withers and Joseph Doddridge, *Notes on the Settlement and Indian Wars* (Wellsburg, Virginia: 1824), had been published when Hildreth and Captain Jolly began their correspondence, and both were based on reminiscences. From time to time Lyman Draper annotated his texts with cross-references to other reminiscences: I have included these annotations here.

As those who have tried to work with his text know, Withers has a tendency to conflate accounts of separate incidents into a single event, and occasionally to make two events out of one. A particular case of the former error occurs in what Jolly took to be an account of the 1781 campaign, but may be a conflation of 1780 and 1782. This matter is dealt with later in this Introduction, under the heading referring to the 1781 Campaign.

In William Darby's words to Lyman Draper, "the Value of such men as Jonathan Zane, Lewis Wetzel, Henry Jolly, Samuel Brady, and many more, of the heroes of those days of danger and blood, was not made up of what they did, in accidental cases to form and adorn a Tale, but in their watchfulness and in the fact, that their names were known and terrible to the savages." [Darby to Draper, August 1, 1845, in *Western Pennsylvania Historical Magazine*, January 1980, p. 39] But of course Captain Jolly's reminiscences deal with what Captain Jolly did, not with his watchfulness, and we must be careful to keep in mind the frontier context in which the price of life was eternal vigilance.

Darby gave Draper the story of how Henry Jolly met his first wife [Darby to Draper, August 19, 1845, in WPHM, Jan. 1980, pp. 43-44, and cf. Mrs. Cruger's Narrative]:

"On the occurrence of one of these Savage alarms, which so often spread desolation, a Mr. [Grice] and family, took refuge in the Fort at Wheeling Forks, but imprudently leaving the shelter too soon, was about a mile or so up Little Wheeling and where the National Road now runs, surprised by savages, part of the family murdered, one son made prisoner, and one Daughter left for dead, being both tomahawked and scalped. She, however, survived her wounds, and became Henry Jolly's first wife. Henry, and Lewis Bonnet, were the men who carried her into the Fort. These two men were then, with Lewis Wetzel and Jonathan Zane, the Heroes of West Virginia."

The Reminiscences are arranged in the Draper MSS according to the dates at which they were written in the let-

ters to Hildreth. In fact 6NN:28, the first part of the reminiscences, was written before the correspondence with Hildreth
began. I have re-ordered them, roughly in chronological
order, though the digression on the Wetzel family, and the
much longer over-all account of the life of Lewis Wetzel, have
presented a problem. My solution has been to place them
after the first Wetzel adventure in the chronological reminiscences (Killbuck and The Tall Pine).

The order in which the Reminiscences are printed is thus
as follows: Draper MSS NN:28(1-4), 6NN:37, 6NN:39-40,
6NN:46-47, 6NN:41-42, 6NN:43-45, 6NN:29-32, 6NN:54-55,
6NN:48, 6N:50-51, 6NN:52-53, 6NN:57-59, 6NN:38, 6NN:60-
61. Roughly speaking, they are in chronological order, with
an excursus on the Wetzel Family *in medias res*. The final
item, printed as a kind of appendix to the Reminiscences, is
Captain Jolly's review of Alexander Withers, *Chronicles of
Border Warfare* (1831), from Draper 6NN:33-36. This repeats
and amplifies portions of the Reminiscences. For clarity, I
have reprinted the passages from Withers to which Jolly
refers, if he does not. Some portions of the early part of the
Reminiscences appear in *Frontier Advance on the Upper Ohio*
(Madison: 1916), from 6NN:28 and (the Henry Children) from
6NN:37. To the best of my knowledge, no other portions have
been published. In any case, I think it well to read the story
through from beginning to end.

THE NARRATIVE OF LYDIA BOGGS SHEPHERD CRUGER

Lydia Boggs Shepherd Cruger was born February 26,
1766, in Berkeley County, Virginia, the daughter of Captain
William Boggs. The family moved to the region of Uniontown,
Pennsylvania, in 1771, and in the spring of 1774 to Charti-
ers, Pennsylvania. Mostly the people at Chartiers "went off"
(in her words), "and a poor crop was made, and corn scarce
and high [in price] the next year." Her Narrative to Lyman
Draper begins with the frontier song, "Brave Lewis Our
Colonel," which has been published in Thwaites, *Dunmore's
War*, (Madison: 1905, reprinted Bowie, MD: Heritage Books

Inc., 1989), pp. 433-435, and is not reprinted here. Though some portions of her account of the siege in 1777 have been printed in *Frontier Defense on the Upper Ohio* (Madison: 1912), pp. 65-68, the entire Narrative is printed here, except for the song. The narrative has, however, been rearranged so that all the portions dealing with each of the chief events -- as, for example, the various sieges of Wheeling -- are printed together. The original text is in Draper 2S: 141-204.

In addition, because this is taken from Draper's notes of conversations, I have thought myself at liberty to insert personal pronouns ("he" or "they") in appropriate places, without using square brackets. The only square brackets used are for questionable readings or the use of my own word to replace an illegible word or a blank.

Mrs. Cruger's use of "Wheeling" for the town that grew up around Fort Henry is anachronistic. In the Heroic Age (Darby's term, you will recall), Wheeling referred only to the Creek and its various branches. These were Indian Wheeling (not strictly speaking a branch, but a separate creek on the Indian side of the Ohio -- in other words, a creek now in the State of Ohio), and the three forks of Wheeling Creek proper, on the (West) Virginia side, Upper, Middle, and Lower Wheeling. The forks of Wheeling were and are several miles inland from the present city of Wheeling, West Virginia, but are within the State of West Virginia.

Lydia Boggs is perhaps best known to historians of the area as the woman who opposed the claim that Betty Zane carried powder to the defenders of Wheeling (Fort Henry) in the Siege of 1782. Since the exploit was ascribed to a member of the leading family of the area, and had become enshrined in folklore (and "history") before she spoke out, Mrs. Cruger brought little but trouble on herself by her opposition. The matter was the subject of discord and disagreement as early as 1824 (when Betty Zane was still alive), and indeed contributed to the failure of Joseph Doddridge to cover the sieges of Wheeling in his *Notes on the Settlement and Indian Wars of the Western Parts of Virginia and Pennsylvania* (Clarksburg: 1824). His MS account, incomplete and not printed there, is included as an Appendix to this volume, thus putting between one set of covers the three major sources for the Indian attack of 1781. It was on account of controversy centering on the 1782 attack, however, that Dr. Doddridge withheld publication of his notes on the sieges of Wheeling.

Briefly, the Zane family through the years, the historians of Wheeling, the citizens of the surrounding area -- including Martinsville, Ohio, where the annual Betty Zane Days are held even now --, have all taken Betty Zane and her exploit to their hearts. Not to mention its promulgation in the novels of her great-grandnephew Zane Grey, including the eponymous *Betty Zane*. When I attended a Zane Grey Society meeting in Norwich, Ohio, back in 1985, there was available a hagiographic pamphlet by the official historian, on Betty Zane. It -- and he -- suggested that Mrs. Cruger had been thwarted in her love (perhaps for Lewis Wetzel) by the superiority of Betty's charms and had never forgiven her. He was a charming conversationalist and I much enjoyed my talks with him, but the pamphlet is chiefly valuable as encapsulated folklore.

The rivalry for the love of Lewis Wetzel is a story almost old enough to be true, but a search of what sources there are (and particularly the *Recollections of Lewis Bonnett, Jr.* -- that is, of Wetzel's cousin) has convinced me that it has little but age to recommend it. Certainly Lyman Draper threw up his hands when he tried to find the truth of the matter, and was reduced to saying despairingly that there might have been parallel events at two of the sieges, which, however, he thought most unlikely, if not impossible. I suppose there could have been two events at the 1782 siege -- Betty Zane and Molly Scott (Mrs. Cruger's heroine) both carrying powder -- but against this idea must be set Mrs. Cruger's denial that Betty Zane was then any closer to Wheeling than the purlieus of Washington, Pennsylvania. I have preferred not to take sides in the matter. Mrs. Cruger's affidavit on the subject is reprinted in Appendix IV, being taken from De Hass, *History and Indian Wars of Western Virginia* (Wheeling: 1851).

Apart from the controversy over the name of the person who carried the powder, which has obscured the real value of Mrs. Cruger's Narrative, there is much in the story Mrs. Cruger tells that merits our attention. In particular, her account of the taunting and insulting remarks passed back and forth between the defenders and attackers, before the attack, reminds me strongly, perhaps irresistibly, of the soldiers before and on the walls of Troy. Even if Mrs. Cruger is remembering with advantages, the similarity of spirit is great. And what is it she says of Jonathan Zane -- that he was too proud to be cooped up in the fort, keeping watch. Darby's "Heroic Age" had much in common with an earlier Heroic Age, as I have noted before.

Yet it is not the 1782 campaign, but the virtually un- known 1781 campaign on which this book adds most greatly to our knowledge. Indeed, when Consul W. Butterfield sought (in his Introduction to the *Washington-Irvine Correspondence*, Madison: 1882) to write an account of this campaign, the sources he used were Henry Jolly, Lydia Cruger, and the brief note by Dr. Doddridge. To these I have added, in a second Appendix, the account written in 1882 by Dr. J. C. Hupp, so far as Lyman Draper thought it worth preserving in his papers. This account, however, differs in several particu- lars from the more contemporary accounts by Jolly and Mrs. Cruger. It may be well here to present an overview of this virtually unknown campaign, involving a force somewhat smaller than the force that attacked Fort Henry the next year, but more successful in death and destruction, if not in victory.

THE 1781 CAMPAIGN AGAINST WHEELING AND LITTLE WASHINGTON

The two sets of reminiscences printed here, with the Doddridge Appendix, provide most of our little knowledge of the 1781 Campaign which has been said to involve an attack on Wheeling, but which was directed more against what is now Washington, Pennsylvania, was then Catfish Camp in the (disputed) District of West Augusta, Virginia, and was for many years known familiarly in the area around about as Little Washington (compare "Little York" for the town of York, Pennsylvania). As noted above, I have added, as a further Appendix, a centennial article by Dr. J. C. Hupp on the Affair at Link's Block House, which has some value as a retelling of a traditional story in the area.

On August 18, 1781, David Zeisberger, the well-known minister at the Moravian missionary town on the Tuscarawas (in what is now Ohio), despatched a message to Colonel Brodhead, at Pittsburgh (Fort Pitt), informing him that a large party of Indians (about 250 in all) was approaching the line of the Ohio, under command of the British Indian agent Matthew Elliot. "They will try to decoy the garrison out where they will lie in ambush," at Fort Henry or perhaps other forts (quoted in Butterfield, *Washington-Irvine Correspondence*, p. 58). The letter was in Brodhead's hands by August 25, 1781, and he notified the commandant at Fort Henry of Zeisberger's news.

The Indians had (according to Henry Jolly) encamped around the Moravian town, "with the purpose of preventing the Moravians from conveying intelligence to the frontier." But "a crippled squaw was permitted to pass out, and conveyed the intelligence to Fort McIntosh [on Beaver Creek, northwest of Fort Pitt], from there to Pittsburgh to Colonel Brodhead," and from there to the frontier.

According to Alexander Scott Withers (*Chronicles of Border Warfare*, Clarksburg: 1831, p. 217), "The Indian army, destined to operate against North Western Virginia, was to enter the country in two divisions of one hundred and fifty warriors each; the one crossing the Ohio near below Wheeling, the other at the mouth of Raccoon creek, about sixty miles farther up. Both were, avoiding the stronger forts, to proceed directly to Washington, then known as Catfish-town." Withers goes on to say that the southern division crossed the Ohio, alarmed the countryside, thus leading the settlers to concentrate their strength at Fort Henry, so that the Indians, balked of their planned success, tied their male prisoners to saplings and tomahawked them (p. 218).

Now the Withers chronology seems to place this in 1780, while the size of the Indian force and the mention of a force also directed against Kentucky seems to place it in 1782. But Captain Jolly took it as referring to the 1781 Campaign, and I think we may fairly conclude that -- since there is no other campaign in which the Indians divided their force in this manner, and since there were many more men on the Tuscarawas than Pekillon commanded -- this is a genuine tradition from the 1781 attack. The fact that Pekillon is recorded as commanding only eighty men rather than one hundred or one hundred and fifty may be explained by a further division of forces, and by the fact that (as Jolly reports) a small force crossed before the main force and then retreated back across the Ohio with plunder.

In any event, only about a third of the Indian force that had been on the Tuscarawas came into the vicinity of Fort Henry, under the command not of Matthew Elliot but of the Delaware Chief Pekillon, considered a friend of the Americans up to that time. When the Indians came near Fort Henry, they found three young boys, about the age of twelve, outside the fort. One was killed, one wounded (but he escaped into the fort), and one captured. The captured boy, David Glenn, told the Indians that the garrison of Fort Henry had been given news of their approach from the commandant at Fort Pitt, who had the information from the Moravian missionaries on the Tuscarawas.

The Indian forces bypassed Fort Henry to the northeastward, and directed their attacks along Buffalo Creek, which flows into the Ohio north of Wheeling. They were to carry out the same maneuver the next year, when beaten back from

Fort Henry. The difference is that in 1781 they moved against the farthest headwaters of the Dutch Fork of Buffalo Creek, while in 1782 they moved against the lower waters of Dutch Fork, where Rice's Fort was located. (See Raymond Bell, *The Dutch Fork Settlement of Donegal Township, Washington County, Pennsylvania.* Washington PA: 1984)

Jolly records that "volunteers immediately turned out to the frontier forts, including a party of twelve from the vicinity of Washington, Pennsylvania (Catfish Camp), which went to Vanmeter's Fort, but hearing that a small band of Indians had seized some horses and killed some hogs and then re-crossed the Ohio, they returned to Washington, only to hear the next day that a larger party had crossed the Ohio at Boggs Island, below Wheeling.

The Indians then struck Middle Wheeling, which had a bend to the southward before the forks, and followed this north. They thus bypassed both Fort Henry and Shepherd's Fort (see map). Reaching the headwaters of Middle Wheeling Creek without incident, though the settlers had spies out, they came upon Link's Blockhouse on Middle Wheeling, which had been abandoned as a fort but which was occupied by a small party of spies or scouts. These were Frank Hupp, Jacob Miller, and perhaps Jonathan Link (included in J. C. Hupp's article but not in the other accounts).

If we are to believe Dr. Hupp's story (which is essentially Jacob Miller's story as handed down), three men slept in the blockhouse that night, and two of them (the other two besides Miller) were killed or mortally wounded when they went out for water in the morning. If we are to believe Henry Jolly, Miller bargained for his life, either before or after the others were killed or mortally wounded. The stories could be conflated, and both may be true. (It occurs to me that this statement may need explanation for readers not immediately familiar with some of the problems of traditional frontier narratives: obviously Miller escaped -- the point on which the narratives differ is the honor of his escape.)

After killing or capturing the men at Link's Blockhouse, the Indians pressed on to the farms of Presley Peak and William Hawkins. Dr. Hupp will have it that Hawkins was captured at Peak's, and Jolly does not say, leaving it to be inferred that he was captured at his own farmstead. These two farms were on the ridge dividing the headwaters of Buffalo Creek from those of Middle Wheeling Creek.

A party of twenty volunteers (including Jolly) passed between the Indians coming from Link's and their objective at Peak's and Hawkins's farms, without detecting them. According to Mrs. Cruger, whose source of information was almost certainly her first husband, Moses Shepherd (b. 1763), Link's wife and child had left the blockhouse with Moses Shepherd and one of the Wetzels, and a snake-bit man who had come from Catfish (that is, "Little Washington"). She has his name as Blackburn, but the others have it as Burnet or Burnett.

The snake-bit man may have been taken at Hawkins's or Peak's -- Mrs. Cruger says at Hawkins's, while Dr. Hupp gives us to understand that both Hawkins and Burnet (the snake-bit man) were taken at Peak's. Since he also gives us to understand that Peak was subsequently tomahawked, while both Jolly and Mrs. Cruger have him carried to Detroit and eventually released, it would appear that Dr. Hupp is at least in part unreliable, though he doubtless repeats the traditional "knowledge" of his time. In any event, the Indians captured Miss Hawkins, who was ill, at her house. They captured Peak at or near his. They captured Burnet (whom we have identified as the "snake-bit man") and William Hawkins. Two or three of the prisoners they tied to trees (we reject Dr. Hupp's supposition that they were seated) and tomahawked, somewhere along the ridge. Two separate parties had attacked the two separate farms, but they had reunited at Peak's before heading for the Ohio.

Mrs. Hawkins and her infant had escaped from the house and hidden first in the woods and then squatting in the stream (presumably Dutch Fork). The Indians, as we have noted, apparently missed her twice, while capturing a Miss Walker and killing Miss Walker's father within her sight or hearing or both. The location of the Hawkins house on a high bluff on the branch of Buffalo Creek aided Mrs. Hawkins in her first escape, enabling her to evade the attentions of the enemy (the full story is given by Jolly).

Jolly has it that Link, Burnet, and Hawkins were toma-hawked: Mrs. Cruger omits Link and has Burnet as Black-burn. Both Mrs. Cruger and Dr. Hupp insist that Hawkins was killed because he had red hair, and Burnet because he was a hairy man (black hair -- is this the origin of Mrs. Cruger's Blackburn?). Jolly has Jacob Link as the third man tomahawked, while Hupp has Peak (who survived) and has Jonathan Link killed at the blockhouse. In any event, Miss Hawkins, Miss Walker, Jacob Miller, and Presley Peak were not tomahawked on the ridge.

Dr. Hupp tells a strange story that the Indians, after the tomahawking, were brought to remorse and moved to the Ohio at the call of a "warbling songster of the wood." Given the Native American use of birdcalls as signals, I suspect that this was a warning signal of the approach of spies or scouts. The Indian party moved on to a camp on the banks of Big Wheeling (this may be Indian Wheeling), from which Miller escaped.

When Mrs. Hawkins and her infant were found, and Mrs. Hawkins told their discoverer, who was one of a party of twenty-five from Catfish, "that she had seen a party, sun about two hours high" the day before. The men immediately rushed off. Let Jolly tell the story:

"'My God, Indians here about two hours ago!' and the whole party appeared panic struck in a moment, and off they went, the fastest horse I believe foremost. I think there was not less than twenty-five of the party, and only two remained to assist the distressed woman. Such were the heroes of Washington County; such were the men who murdered the

Moravians; such were the men that Colonel Williamson mostly commanded."

THE EFFECTS OF THE 1781 CAMPAIGN

Besides the deaths of William Hawkins, Link, and Burnet, and the captivities of Miss Elizabeth Hawkins and Presley Peak -- and perhaps of Miss Walker who seems to disappear from the story -- there were three notable results of the small-scale 1781 campaign. By the way, Peak spent some-time under British guard (or protection) at Detroit, before returning to the Ohio. Miss Hawkins married a Frenchman (possibly part Native American) at Detroit and remained with him till his death, then returned to the Ohio, but returned again to her husband's country after a few years. According to Hupp's notes, she married into the tribe of her Shawnee captors in the interior of Ohio, and Mrs. Cruger has her return after her visit to her semi-barbarous life.

These stories are not contradictory. My seventh great-grandfather was a part-white Shawnee in the Ohio Country, in a war centered on Detroit, and I daresay, for all that he was part Irish (and perhaps Spanish), his life was semi-barbarous.

The least of the three results of the campaign was the revelation of the cowardice (in Jolly's view) of the men from Catfish Camp. This prefigured the revulsion of the settlers to the westward at the murder of the Moravian Indians by these same men under Colonel David Williamson (1753-1809) later on, but it had little long-run effect in and of itself. The presence of Pekillon, who was not a Moravian but was linked to them in the public mind, led to a conviction among many of the settlers that they had been attacked by Moravians. This supported the desire of Williamson's men to take re-venge on the Moravians, which they did, although their actions were apparently opposed by Jacob Miller, who had been captured by Pekillon's men. (The story is in Jolly's reminiscences.)

The information provided by the captive boy from Fort Henry, young David Glenn, led to the breaking up of the Moravian mission on the Tuscarawas. The missionaries, Zeisberger and Heckewelder, were taken to Detroit, interrogated, and eventually released. The Moravian Indians followed their own trail of tears to Upper Sandusky, and there starved. Some came back to their former settlement, to seek a harvest from the frozen soil, and to find death, bereft of their missionary protection, at the hands of Williamson's men (a brave man, Jolly says, but "with a degree of cruelty very unbecoming a soldier").

One by-product of Glenn's information was the Indian belief in 1782 that there was only a wooden cannon at Fort Henry, whereas a swivel-gun from Pittsburgh had been brought there between the 1781 campaign and the siege in 1782. This doubtless had its effect on Indian morale in 1782 -- if they expected a log cannon, a real one would have a shattering effect. Mrs. Cruger reports the British reaction to the presence of the swivel-gun.

THE NEXT DRAPER SOCIETY PUBLICATIONS

The next publications will include the longer of the two accounts of the captivity of the Henry children, and the narrative of George Edgington, complementing that of Major Lewis Bonnett, Jr., in our first volume. Also, we hope to publish, separately, an edited version of Lyman Copeland Draper's history of the first conflict of the settlers and Indians in the Valley of Virginia (1742), in the 250th year from that clash, tentatively titled: *Action at the Galudoghson.*

Further down the road are the War of 1812 Letters of Lt. Col. George Croghan, two early (1790s) narratives of Marietta and Cincinnati, and Lyman Draper's account of the Big Sandy Expedition of 1756 and its officers.

For their help (whether intended or not) in preparing this volume, besides William Darby, Dr. Samuel Hildreth, and

Lyman Copeland Draper, I owe thanks to several others in more modern times. I wish to thank Bryan Costello and David Zincavage for their aid in deciphering and transcribing these reminiscences and H. Nicholas Muller III and the State Historical Society of Wisconsin for permission to publish them. I would also like to thank Bill Thompson, for many years the Historian of the State of Wisconsin, for his assistance and encouragement over the years, and Stacia Straley Costello for introducing me to the heritage and history of the Upper Ohio.

Jared C. Lobdell
New Haven, Connecticut
December 1991

Narrative of Indian and Tory Depradations in Pennsylvania 1770-1777 by John Crawford (1772-1831)

Y GRANDFATHER JOHN Crawford was an immigrant from Scotland and settled and improved a tract of land near where Chambersburgh now stands, where he died in the year 1740, leaving a widow, four sons, and one daughter, namely George, Arthur, William (my father), Mary, and John, who was a posthumous child. The widow afterwards married John McKinney (who was likewise an emigrant from Scotland), by whom she had three sons and one daughter, namely James, Robert, Joseph, and Elizabeth. John McKinney sold the plantation near Chambersburgh and removed to Big Kanalloway near where Hancock Town now stands, where shortly afterwards his house was burned by Indians and himself taken prisoner. The family bible was burned in the house, in which the children's ages were recorded.

THE CAPTURE OF JOHN MCKINNEY

McKinney knew the Indian that took him. They had a long race, and when the Indian took hold of him, he says, John you run very fast, and you run a great while too. The Indian's name I have forgotten: however, McKinney called him by name, and says, I hope you will not kill me. The Indian said he would not and kept his word. He was taken to Fort Duquesne (now Pittsburgh), and from there to Canada, where the French set him to reaping peas with three other fellow prisoners. This was near the St. Lawrence, or probably Niagara.

However, one night, after working hard all day, the four prisoners took a canoe and made their escape over the river, and after many days made their way to the settled parts of the State of New York. I do not recollect how many days they were in the wilderness, but I remember to hear that shortly after they made their escape, John McKinney had the misfortune to have his shoulder dislocated, and [it] was not put in till he came to the settlement. They suffered greatly for provisions, having nothing but what they could pick up in the woods. One article of food was a hawk that had stuck his claws into a fish and was unable to raise with it or to extricate himself from it. They killed both the fish and the hawk. When opening the hawk, he found in it a snake, but still they ate it. Pinching hunger made it palatable.

When they came within a short distance of the settlement, they disputed about the course. McKinney and one of the men took one direction and [the] other two a different one. The whole party by this time was nearly exhausted with hunger and fatigue, and had nearly given themselves up to despair, but fortunately the two men that had parted from McKinney came to the settlement early the next day and gave an account of their unfortunate companions who separated from them the day before, on hearing which a number of the inhabitants started in search of them and found them. From the course they were going, they never would have reached the settlement in their enfeebled condition.

The man who found them was obliged to carry them part of the way to the settlement. On their arrival, a doctor was procured to put in the shoulder of McKinney, which I think my father had told me had been out eleven days. He bathed it for a long time with warm water before he put it in. I do not know whether this is a practice with the doctors of the present day; however, his shoulder was put in and McKinney was treated with the greatest kindness by the people and returned to his family exactly in eleven months from the day he was taken.

THE CAPTURE OF ARTHUR CRAWFORD

Arthur Crawford, my father's brother, was taken prisoner about the same time but by a different party of Indians. I have heard my father say he was about 14 years of age when he was taken and that he was two years older than my father, who was born on the 6th of August 1744. From this he must have been taken about 1756. When McKinney came in he brought the news that Arthur Crawford was living and that he had seen him at Fort Duquesne, that he was amongst the Dellaway nation of Indians.

The circumstance of the capture of Arthur Crawford was as follows: (to wit), he was in company with his uncle of name of Lowther, his first name I have forgotten, when the Indians came upon them. Lowther having a rifle, he shot down one of the Indians, after which they were both taken. Lowther was stripped naked and tied to a cabin. Arthur Crawford was tied to a tree at a short distance, where he could see all that was going on. There had been a number of reapers at the place who had left syckles hanging on the corner of the cabin. Those syckles the Indians took and amused themselves for about an hour in cutting Lowther in every part of his body and limbs. They put out both his eyes with the points of the syckles, and when they had thus satisfied their hellish vengeance, they tomahawked, scalped him, and cut off his head.

Arthur Crawfold, after seeing these horrid cruelties practiced on his uncle, was taken to Fort Duquesne, as I have before stated, and was adopted into the family of the noted Indian Chief White Eyes. This White Eyes afterwards embrace[d] the Christian religion and had a son educated at Princeton College, New Jersey.

About the time of the capture of Arthur Crawford, there was one Thomas Lynn tomahawked and scalped by the Indians, and left for dead. My father was on a hill at some distance and seen the whole transaction. Lynn recovered but lost his sight. Isaac Lynn, the brother of Thomas, was taken at the same time. He was about the age of my uncle Arthur Crawford, and after they had been prisoners several years, they agreed to run away from the Indians together, but Lynn had become so attached to the Indians that he divulged the secret and had like to have cost my uncle his life.

White Eyes, my uncle's Indian father, took all the skins of my uncle's killing for the first two years. After that he let him hunt for himself, and he became the greatest hunter and trapper of his day, particularly in hunting with the stocking head. This mode of hunting I have never seen put in practice, but it has been described to me by my father, thus: when the buck is killed and the horns in full bloom, take the whole head and horns with some of the joints of the neck, and over this draw a stocking or piece of cloth the colour of the deer's hair at the hunting season, so as to represent the neck of the buck. The hunter hides himself in the bushes, or behind a tree, and holds to fair view the head and horns of the buck, and works with it in such a way that the deer is deceived in the appearance and will walk up frequently so near that the hunter can strike him with his hand.

This mode of hunting has been laid aside before my time, or at least I have not seen it put in practice, but I have been told that a Michael DeBolt that lived about five miles from my father's when I was a child did practice it. He had been a long time prisoner with the Indians. I think when the Indians used nothing but bows and arrows, this mode would be very important.

Arthur Crawford continued to live with the Indians for seven years, but might have come home to his people at the end of six years had not fortune decided otherwise. The case is thus. He had his hunting or Indian cabin at the mouth of Big Beaver on the Ohio, and he had skins and furs sufficient to have loaded his two horses. In the Spring of the year he started on a trapping tour up Big Beaver, intending on his return to start home. But on his return, behold the Ohio had raised so high in his absence as to carry off his cabin and all his skins, and as he had reason to believe (which was really true) that his friends were all poor, he concluded to stay and hunt another year and came in with his two horses loaded with skins.

THE RETURN OF ARTHUR CRAWFORD

When he came home, his mother was dead and the family scattered. My father had been bound by the orphan's court, and was living with Samuel Combs in Loudon County, Virginia. How my father came to be so far removed from his former place of residence I have never learned. Pontiack's war breaking out shortly after the return of Arthur Crawford, he was commissioned Captain of a ranging company and the people had great expectations from his services, but in this they were disappointed, for shortly afterwards he caught the smallpocks and died, together with his sister Mary. My father never seen his brother Arthur after his return from the Indians. It is true his master gave him liberty to go and see his brother within the Christmas holidays, but with positive orders to be back within a certain time, but on account of high waters he was detained and obliged to return without seeing his brother, and the next news he heard was that he was dead.

My uncle John Crawford was with my uncle Arthur from the time of his return from the Indians to his death,and it is from him that I have learned more of the anecdotes of my uncle Arthur. He says my uncle Arthur was about five feet eight inches high, square built, and very active and strong; that he could carry a large buck on his back for several miles with great ease; that shortly after he was taken by the Indians, his Indian father (White Eyes) had his hunting camp near where Brownsville now stands; and that in the morning when Arthur was starting out to hunt, White Eyes would give him as much sausage stuft in bear's gut as he would lap round his fingers and tell him, Boys must not eat much, for if they did, they would never make good hunters.

My uncle was usually fortunate in hunting, but there was another Indian in their company that had a son about the age of my uncle. He would frequently come to camp at night and bring in no game. His father would apply a hickory to his back (a practice very uncommon with the Indians) and tell him he did not hunt right; he kept too much on the water courses, whereas he ought to hunt on the tops of the ridges.

About this time, George Crawford, my father's oldest brother, started on a visit to see some friends in North Carolina, and was drowned in James River, Virginia.

MY FATHER, WILLIAM CRAWFORD

My father, William Crawford, served out his time with Samuel Combs, except the last five months when an argument took place between him and his master that my father was to have liberty to depart on condition that his master was to be exonerated from paying any freedom dues. My father then [en]listed for five months under Captain Chamel, a Scotchman who was commissioned to raise a company of rangers to defend the frontier. Their headquarters was at Enoch's Fort on Big Capecapon. They were dressed in the fashion of the Scotch highlanders with the plaid or kilt.

My father was married to the daughter of David Kennedy near the forks of Conoquige and came to the western country in the year 1769, and made a small improvement, and returned in the year 1770. He came out with an intention of continuing the said improvement, but when he came to the spot he found one Roger Roberts at work on the land, and wishing to have no dispute he sold Roberts his improvement for a trifle, and came to the west side of the Monongahela River, and with his Negro man named Cook, he began an improvement.

They had brought with them one cow to give them milk. They built a cabin, cleared five acres of ground, and put in corn. As my father had a rifle, he killed as much wild meat as he wanted for himself. My uncle John Crawford came out at the same time and improved land adjoining. After my father had laid by his corn, he hired Cook to William Shepherd, who with his wife had moved out the same Spring, and his wife Rebekah Shepherd was the only white woman then in the bounds of what is now Greene County.

The distance from Shepherd's cabin to my father's was about three miles. Cook was to come every Saturday afternoon to see the corn. My father started over the mountain to move out my mother and my oldest sister, which was all the child they had at the time. My father at the mouth of Muddy Creek met Thomas Crago, an old acquaintance from Conoquige. He told my father he had two cows, that they gave him plenty of milk and could make butter if he had a churn. My father gave him directions where to find his cabin, and to take his churn and keep it till his return from over the mountain.

INDIAN DEPRADATIONS

Accordingly, Crago in a few days came to the cabin and took the churn, and on his return was met by four Indians, two men and two women. These Indians attempted to take Crago's horse to carry one of their party who had been wounded shortly before, on the Monongahela River near the laurel point by some whitemen from whom they had stole some property.

As they were descending the river, Crago would not give up his horse. A scuffle took place. Crago got the Indian down and one of the Indian women took a rifle and shot Crago through the head. The next day old Koock came to see the corn in company with John Moore, and when they came within three fourths of a mile of my father's cabin, they came upon the dead body of Crago, and my father's churn lay by him. Moore left his gun with Cook to watch the corpse and gathered some of the neighbours, buried Crago, and followed the Indians to where they had camped the night before.

They had not taken the horse more than half a mile till they tomahawked him, and at their camp they had tomahawked a dog, to keep [it] from barking as was supposed. After burying Crago, the party charged Kook not to tell Mrs. Shepherd that the Indiasns had killed Crago, as she was the only white woman in the country, which he promised to observe, but when he returned, Mrs. Shepherd asked him if he had seen anything of Thomas Crago. He made no answer. She asked him a second time, and a third time, and still no answer. She then asked him if the Indians had killed him. His answer then was that men had told him not to tell her. This was telling her plain enough. A lie was unnatural to Cook. The last part of the foregoing tale I had from Mrs. Shepherd's own mouth in last June, 1831, for she is still living and perfectly intelligible, though upwards of eighty years of age.

The reasons Mrs. Shepherd gave me for thinking the Indians killed Thomas Crago was as follows: Crago had as yet built no cabin, but with his two little boys (Thomas and Robert) lived in a camp by the side of a log. The oldest boy was eleven, the younger nine years of age. The youngest boy, Robert, had got his hand burned and every morning for some time had come to Mrs. Shepherd's to get his hand dressed. The morning after their father was killed, [the] boys came as usual to get Robert's hand dressed. They told Mrs. Shepherd "Daddy has run away." "Where has he run to?" says Mrs. Shepherd. The boys said he had the day before went to Bill Crawford's to get a churn and had not returned. From that moment Mrs. Shepherd thought the Indians had killed him, for certainly he would not have left those little boys all night by themselves.

About this time an Indian by the name of Bald Eagle had been hunting high up the Monongahela River, and after making his hunt was ascending the Monongahela River with his skins, when about four miles below where Morgan Town now stands, he was fired upon by a young man of the name of J. S. [Scott -- LCD] and killed without any provocation whatever. The canoe with the dead Indian floated down to Provence's Fort about two miles above the mouth of Big Whitely, where he was taken out and buried, but what became of his skins I never learned.

Sometime after this, other Indians on their way down the river called on D. S., the uncle of J. S. who had killed their friend Bald Eagle. He told them there was bad people at Provence's Fort: it would be best for them not [to] call there. Accordingly, when they passed Provences Fort they kept on the opposite side of the river.

About this time an Indian by the name of Jacob, with his family, lived on Kelm's Fork of Dunkard. He tended a small patch of rock bottom land in corn, and hunted. He continued there for some time and was very serviceable to the white people living on the lower parts of Dunkard, by furnishing them with many horse loads of wild meat at a moderate price. At length some lawless men whose names I have forgotten came to [his] cabin and murdered him. [This occurred early in September 1769 -- LCD.] Two of his children made their escape to the Ohio, where they found some other Indians when they were almost starved to death. It gives me pain to state those things, but truth requires it should be done.

Notwithstanding the universal disposition of the Indians to retaliate for an injury done to an individual of their tribe, there was as yet no war, but in the Spring of 1774, when Cresap and Greathouse with their party killed a number of peaceable Indians (the particulars of which are stated in Jefferson's *Notes of Virginia*), the people instantly set about building Forts in every direction on both sides of the Monongahela River, with the full expectation that there would be an Indian War.

LOGAN

In this they were not disappointed, for in May 1774 the noted Indian chief Logan came with a party and killed a man by the name of Spicer with his wife and five children, and took two of his children prisoner, to wit: Betsy, a girl of eleven years, and William, nine years old.

As soon as my father received the alarm, he took my mother and [the] children to Jenkins Fort and then rode all night to warn the people to fly to the forts for safety. The next day my father went with a party to bury the dead. The sight was awful to those who had never seen anything of the kind before, but to my father those scenes had been common from his childhood. One man says, For God's sake let us clear ourselves: the Indians are hiding in the high weeds near us, and will kill us every one. My father says, For God's sake, do you clear yourself: such a man as you is sufficient to spoil a dozen good men!

Captain Logan sent on the prisoners and plunder with the main body of the Indians from the place where he killed the family, which was on a branch of Dunkard Creek called Meadow Run, and himself and an Indian of the name of Snake, and they two came on to Big Whitely Creek and killed a man by the name of Kenar who was not found for several days, till the buzzards was seen flying about his dead body. When he was taken up and buried, those two Indians secreted themselves behind a fence near Jenkins fort, the same evening after the party had returned from burying Spicer's family.

The following narrative I will give as Betsy Spicer had it from Captain Logan on his return to the Indian Towns. He says, when lying behind the fence, he heard a woman with a sharp shrill voice say, Who will turn out and guard the women to milk the cows. There was, he said, a long string of men came out of the fort gate with rifles on their shoulders, and when they came out they were fequently pointing with their rifles at different objects. Several times they pointed towards him, and he had sometimes thought of running, but laid still till night.

When him and his comrade Snake went off the next day, they came on the waters of Muddy Creek to the cabin of James Flenikin, where they killed a mare and a pet wolf, from thence to the cabin of John Crawford (my uncle), where they cut some bags of rye to pieces and took a brass kettle, which they took only about three hundred yards, when they stuck a tomahawk through its bottom and left it. From thence they went to the cabin of Thomas Hughes, where they broke some potmetal. From thence they came to the cabin of James Moredock, but took nothing but a plate of meat. From thence they came near Vanmeter's Fort, where they killed a man of the name of Wall.

There was some mischief done about this time on the waters of Tenmile, but I am not sure these two Indians did it. The same day that those depradations were committed, my father with his black man Cook and an Irish weaver of the name of John Sloan started to my father's cabin to bring some necessaries and drive out a cow to give milk to his children (I was the youngest). When they came to my father's cabin and loaded the horses, Cook mounted one, John Sloan the other, each with his clasp knife open in his hand, intending if fired upon by the Indians to cut the lash ropes and let the loads tumble, and clear themselves on horse back if possible.

My father says, John, do you think you could fight? Ah, God (says John), I have fought on board of a 74 till the blood run out o' our scuttles. They took up the line of march, the cavalry in front, my father in the rear with his rifle, driving the cow before him. When the party came near my uncle John Crawford's cabin, it seems the cow seen the Indians, for she run back. My father followed her round my uncle's field and brought her back, and when the party came to the cabin, it had been plundered by the Indians but a moment before!

The door was open, the bags of rye cut in slivers and the rye running out, the brass kettle missing which at that time was all the household furniture, probably, my uncle had left in his cabin. My uncle was not yet married, and in those days, when a man left his cabin, in the language of the New Testament, he took up his bed and walked.

HORSE THIEVES

I should have informed the reader before this, that is, if ever this production should be thought worth reading (which is very doubtful), that my father, when he came to this country, he had three very valuable horses. Three land jobbers, alias horse thieves, came and stayed all night with my father. He gave them the best his cabin afforded, and when they went away they stole all his horses! In the course of some years, one of them was hanged in some parts of Virginia, I have forgot the county. His name was Dilts. He confessed under the gallows that the first horses he ever stole was the property of a man of the name of Crawford in Muddy Creek settlement, that Moses Hollady was in his company, with another man whose name I shall not mention, that they all three had been well treated, that after he had catched the horses his conscience smote him and he turned them loose.

Moses Hollady then called him a damned henhearted son of a bitch and told him to catch the horses again. He did so. All this was no proof against Hollady, but my father thought him guilty, and meeting with him at Catfish's Camp (now Washington) in the [year] 1781-2, he attempted to inflict such punishment as was common in those days, but the Publican protected him by locking him up in the room so that my father could not get at him. At the mouth of Big Sandy on the Ohio in the year 1797 I seen the same Moses Hollady. Two men that I knew was bringing him up the Ohio in a canoe. He was struck with the palsy. He could not walk without crutches and was then a beggar, and presented to me his brief.

I gave him 25 cents and told him, I am the son of such a man living in such a place; now go and sin no more. In the course of that summer he came into the house of my oldest sister living on Big Redstone. He presented his brief. Begone out of my house, you old villain! You stole my father's horses! says my sister. This is the last I heard of Moses Hollady.

THE WAR

During the year 1775-6 I am not positive that there was any murder committed by the Indians, but if I should be better informed, I will state it hereafter. In those years I think the Indians were in suspense whether to join the British or remain neutral. The British wished the Indians to adopt the first, and the United States the latter. However, there was several false alarms. I remember on in the summer of 1776; I was then not four years old -- the particulars of the alarm I do not recollect.

John Blair and family, James Flenikin and family, my father and family, and Uncle John Crawford and family, all fled together to Jenkins Fort, a distance of four miles. I remember I was waked up out of my sound sleep and thrown on a horse behind John Blair, and he carried his little daughter before him. We all arrived at the fort at break of day. On my way to the fort I fell asleep, and in going upon the bank of Little Whitely Creek, I fell off into the bed of the creek. My father was close behind and threw me on again. When we arrived at the fort, and my father and the rest was busy in taking the loads off the horses, I remember to hear my father say, "There is the man that raised the false alarm, "I have a notion to hickory him." However, I seen my father shortly afterwards talking with the man and appeared to be moderate. The man told him he had not told a lie, but he was deceived. I think from the sound of his voice he was a Dutchman. The next day we all came home again.

In the Spring of the year 1777, the Indians committed some depradations which I shall relate hereafter. My father moved his family to Jacob Vanmeter's fort, a distance of three miles, where we remained for about two weeks, when my father moved us home again. When we came home, there was a number of the neighbours collected and was busy in building a fort at my father's. They built five cabins in addition to two others that my father had built for his own convenience. The vacancy between the cabins was filled with stockade, extending about ten feet above the ground, with portholes to fire out of if necessary.

THE TORY YEAR

This year is designated by the name of the Tory Year. It was in this year that so many of my father's neighbours found a conspiracy against the Government, and secretly took an oath to be true to the Government of George the Third, in pointed violation of the Declaration of Independence. I shall tread as lightly on the ashes of those deluded men as will be consistent with truth. I shall only mention the two first letters of the names of those concerned, and although they had threatened the life of my father, yet I have more sympathy for them than for those fallen Americans who before and at the time of our late war [1812 -- JCL] had the audacity to publish to the world that it was a war of aggression [on] our part; that it was an unjust, unnecessary, and cruel war on our part. Oh shame, where is thy blush?

The British Navy had impressed many thousands of our seafaring citizens and made them fight against a nation with whom we were at peace. Those unfortunate men frequently tried to make their escape and on being caught were invariably tied up and whipt, and amongst those illfated men were the two nephews of General Washington. They were of the name of Lewis. One of the brothers deserted twice and was taken each time and twice whipped. The other brother deserted once and was once whipt. Could this good old patriot [have] spoken from the grave, what would have been his indignation? But what will not party spirit produce in a free country, where every man is at liberty to speak and write what he pleases?

But I will return to the Tories of 1777. At this time our struggle with Great Britain was very doubtful. Our northern army had retreated from the walls of Quebeck to the back parts of the State of New York. Tyconderoga had fallen into the hands of the enemy without a struggle. The Indians that had heretofore been wavering now took part against us. Their mode of warfare was an indiscriminate slaughter of all ages and sexes. We had no publick roads, nothing but paths leading from one cabin to another, and of course no publick mail, no news papers to inform us how our friends were coming on with the common enemy. All we heard was from travellers or from our own people returning from Hagerstown or Winchester packing their [horses]. All our information was seldom correct. The Whig would make it a little better and the Tory a little worse than it really was.

In this state of suspense, the stoutest hearts trembled for the fate of America, but at this time we had the Revd. John Coibly settled among us. His prayers and his sermons tended to reanimate the feeble; his preaching was attended by large assemblies. Many would go ten miles to hear him. He represented our cause as the cause of Heaven!

There was likewise at this time a sermon printed in a pamphlet by the Revd. David Jones, a Baptist preacher. I have not seen it for fifty years, but I remember the text. Fight manfully for your wives and your children and your household goods. I remember likewise that he compared the terms of unconditional submission which was offered by Great Britain to the colonies, to that of the terms offered by Nahash the Ammonite to the people of Jabesh Gilead (1st Samuel, Chapter 11, Verse 2nd), which was that Nahash was to [thrust out] the right eye of every man of Jabesh Gilead and lay it for a reproach on all Israel. The inference he drew from this passage [was] that we could trust nothing to the benevolence of the parent country, that we must trust in God and our own abilities to resist the common enemy.

In the Spring of 1777, there were very few disaffected people in our part of the country. Even A. J. [Aaron Jenkins -- LCD], who was afterwards considered and treated as a leading Tory, was a warm Whig. But the Daemon of discord was shortly after this let loose. The British agents came into our country like wolves in sheep's clothing. They represented our cause as hopeless, that if we were conquered with arms in our hands our lives would be endangered, and at all events the lands of the Whigs would be forfeited to the crown.

About this time, a man of the name of Smith from the State of Delaware (the hotbed of Toryism) came to the fort of A. J. [Aaron Jenkins -- LCD] and continued there three or four days. Shortly before this A. J. was on the verge of fighting at fisticuffs with one of the men that lived in the fort with him on the subject of Whig and Tory. This was J. B., a hatter who had a shop in one of the fort cabins. He was an emigrant from England and like many others of his countrymen he sucked in the love of his King with his mother's milk. He was a Tory from principle and perhaps the only one at that time in the country.

Shortly after this, Smith left the fort. A. J. began to alter his tone. He had two fine plantations as any in the country. The thoughts of losing them was dreadful to him. The people began to hold secret meetings in the night. My father shortly after this had some conversation with A. J. and some others of his friends. They gave him reasons to suspect them of Toryism, but in the latter part of July my father was mowing in the meadow of one John Vantress in company with James Mundle. They fell into conversation on the subject of Whig and Tory. My father told Mundle he thought A. J. and a number of his neighbours were Tory. Mundle addressed my father as follows:

William, I wish you would be cautious how you express yourself. The times are critical. It is very uncertain how the contest between us and Britain will end, and I have heard your life threatened. On this my father threw down his scythe with greatest indignation, and says, Who threatens my life? Mundle refused to tell him, but declared he was my father's friend. My father called several men that was mowing in the same meadow at some distance. They came. When my father told them, my neighbour Mundle told me there is a number [of people threatening my life].

Mundle became alarmed for his own safety and saw that A. J. and a number of others, whose names he mentioned were the men that he had seen in the fort of A. J., was knowing [he came] to their meetings and overheard this much, that when their affairs came to a crisis, they would be obliged to dispatch my father and two others, (to wit) Captain John Miner (now Judge Miner) and the Revd. John Corbly, a good old Baptist preacher whose family fell a sacrifice to the Indian tomahawk about five [years] afterwards.

JOHN MASON

In a few days after this, John Mason, a German blacksmith, came to my father's and appeared much alarmed. He addressed my father was follows:

Billy, this day, the morrow, or the Saturday, I must die. He says, This morning I was called by neighbour W., who appeared in great distress, and said, John, I wish to tell you something, but I have sworn not to tell you, but you will be killed in three days, and he shed tears in abundance. Mason says, You say you wish to tell me something and you have sworn not to tell me. You have not sworn not to tell my horse (there was a horse hitched at the smith shop): you can tell him. The simple honest old Dutchman told the horse in presence of Mason that General Burgoyne was to send a part of his army and take Fort Pitt, and the Indians was to take Wheeling on the same day. Then the Tories was to declare themselves for the King, and those who refused to do so would be put to death.

As this was a matter of great importance, and as Mason spoke the English language very imperfectly, my father thought he might not perfectly understand him. He thought proper to go with him to a James Carmichael, who could speak Dutch, but it was found my father had understood him perfectly. Carmichael concluded to go home with Mason. The distance was about six miles, and he went to the house of W. and stayed all night with him, and affected to be a Tory. By this means he got all out of him that he wanted.

The next day he went to the foot of the mountain to Colonel Gaddis and Major Springer, who as soon as possible raised about forty mounted men with a view of inquiring into these matters, but from the thinness of the settlements at that time, so many men could not be collected in a day. The Tories got word of what was going on, for by this time they had partizans everywhere, and prepared to meet their adversaries in bloody combat. The first night after Gaddis and Springer got their men collected, they came to Provences Fort [nearly opposite the mouth of Big Whitely -- LCD] on the east bank of the Monongahela River and [encamped]there the first   •
night. The Tories were collected to the number of one hundred at the distance of one and a half miles and had chosen their officers.

Early in the morning, Major Springer went down to the river to wash himself, when he seen a man a-riding up the beach on the opposite side of the river on a sorrel steed horse. When he came opposite to where the Whig party was camped, he turned about and went off under whip. Springer run up the bank and told his men, Get up your horses as quick as possible -- we are discovered! They marched instantly towards the Tory assembly. When they came within a quarter of a mile, they found one of the Tories that was on the lookout. This man they took prisoner.

This was F. G., the brother of L. G., one of the Tory captains. Captain J. B. was the other captain (not the hatter). The arrangement of the Tories was that Captain L. G. was to fire the first gun. This he says he intended to do, but Col. Gaddis that had taken off his brother prisoner, on his advance to the Toriers had put F. G. in front. He says he could not fire for fear of killing his brother. This was an excuse for cowardice, for when the Whig party came within point blank shot of the Tories, and although the Tories had 100 men and Gaddis but 40 Whigs, the Tories broke and ran without firing a single gun. Many of them run into a cornfield which was eighty perches long and twenty-five perches wide. Gaddis and Springer formed their party in such manner that every man took a certain number of rows of corn and marched from one end of the field to the other, in which they found twelve Tories hid among the corn and pumpkin vines.

About nine o'clock this day I was in the meadow of my father. The grass was cut but some of the hay not yet taken up. I saw a man a-riding along the lane under full whip. It was James Mundle, the man who had notified my father shortly before this that his life was threatened. I ran to the fort with all speed, expecting the hear news of Indians, but all that Mundle knew was that a large body of Tories was collected to oppose Gattis, that from their number in all probability Gaddis would be defeated unless he was reinforced in short time.

In this day of deep distress my father had four men in the fort with him. Two of them were Whigs and two of them were Tories and had at that time taken the oath to the King, but my father had never suspected them. He had two neighbours of the name of [Elias and James -- LCD] Flenikin. These men he knew to be stanch Whigs. He sent one of the Tories to tell the Flenikins to come to him as soon as possible. The Tory done his errand but did not return. The other Tory slipped out and they both went off and found the Tories.

On this day there was thirty men to meet at the house of Captain Pigman to march to Wheeling fort, as that fort was expected to be attacked by the Indians, as related by the honest old Dutch Tory, W. My father thought it prudent to warn Pigman and his party of the enemies nearer home, the Tories. Accordingly, my father and his four neighbours went to Pigman's. Captain Pigman was an active man in defense of the country. On hearing what was going on, the whole went to Swan's Fort, taking every man. As he went along, he addressed them in this manner:

There is at this time a large portion of our fellow citizens in arms against the country, and there must be no skulking between parties. We will take you as friends or enemies, and the choice lies with yourselves. On this representation no man hesitated, but all turned out from Swan's Fort. They marched to meet the Tories not knowing as yet what had been the fate of Gaddis and his party, but when they met with him the Tories, poor fellows, were scattered to the four winds and no doubt were crying to the rocks and mountains to cover them from the vengeance of the Whigs.

AT MY FATHER'S FORT

I will now return to my father's fort. One of the Tories in my father's fort had a wife but no children. The other was a young man. My father and his little party had been gone but a few hours when two women came to move away the Tory's wife. There was a good deal of whispering among the women, and my mother became jealous that there was mischief a-brewing and insisted to know what was the [reason] that the Tory's wife was going away, for as yet the Toryism of her husband had never been suspected. The women cried but would give no satisfaction. My mother threatened to keep them and their horses in the fort unless they could give some better account of themselves.

One of the women says, There is Johnny Provence's mare outside of the fort gate. I will take her and I will bring men enough in short time that will make you glad to let us go. My mother met her at the fort gate with the bat staff in her hand and says, If you advance one step farther I will split your brains out. The old Dutch woman gave back.

However, some time afterwards, my mother agreed to let them go. I seen them start. I remember that they had some part of their plunder on a cow. When they had left the fort but a short distance, one of the women hollo'ed back to my mother that the forest should be in ashes before the next morning.

This threat was truly alarming to the women and children. There was not a man in the fort except poor old lame Cook, and not a single gun and no one to use it if we had one, for I should not have been afraid to let Kook shoot at me fifty yards, and if he had hit me it would have been an accident. In this state of things the women concluded to leave the fort to its fate and accordingly they called an old mare which was all the horse beast on the plantation. On her they put a packsaddle and as much plunder as she could carry, and the rest was left to the mercy of the Tories.

Reader, figure to yourself four or five women with three or four children each bidding a last farewell to the little property they possessed and seeking shelter in some remote spot to save the lives of themselves and their children. I know there will be many of the rising generation that will doubt the facts that I shall relate, but truth is my end and aim. Some of the children was able to walk; the others were carried by the women. We went to an out of the way cabin of a young man by the name of Armstrong. The man was gone with the rest of his neighbours to quail the Tories. His sister kept house for him.

She made us all welcome. As soon as it was dark, the children was put to sleep on the floor. As soon as this was done, my mother and my aunt came back to the fort. They took blankets out of the fort and laid [them] on [a] rising piece of ground about fifteen perches from the fort, expecting every moment to see the fales rise, but in the morning all was safe. They milked the cows and then returned to their children. This day no word from our friends. All was doubt.

The second night my mother and aunt came back and watched as they had done the preceeding night, but shortly after their return the next morning, an old midwife by the name of Margaret McDowell came to us. She told us we might go home with safety, that the Whig party had many Tories in irons, and that no blood had been shed. The place where the Tories were confined [was] at William Miner's fort on Big Whitely.

HUNTING TORIES

When my father met Colonel Gaddis, he was appointed a sergeant and was sent out to catch Tories, with orders if he could not find them to drive off their cattle. This was done in some cases. Early one morning my father got sight of one of the Tory captains, J. B. [Belchy -- LCD]. It was at a place on Big Whitely near where George Reppert's mill now stands. The captain seen my father after him. The captain, by throwing away his gun, outran my father for the present. However, in the afternoon of the same day, my father discovered the captain with three other men with guns, and a woman, all setting on a log. They saw nothing of him. The weeds were high and he crawled on his hands and knees till he got so close to them that if he would stand up straight his shadow would reach them.

When he sprang up and presented his rifle, and says, The first man that makes the least resistance, I'll blow his brains out, they gave a faint scream and raised about half up, but sat down again and said they would give up. My father says, Ground your arms and march three paces from them. They did so. My father took up their guns and ordered them to march on before him. They obeyed him. Their spirits were sunk, if they ever had any, for surely it was fear that induced them to enter into the conspiracy in the first instance.

My father marched them before him for about half a mile to the place. He blew upon his powder a charge, which was the signal agreed upon. In a short time his men came to him, and then the following conversation took place between my father and the Tory captain. My father says, Captain B., you and me had a smart race this morning. Yes, says the Captain, I was very much scared. It is a great pity that a captain should be so frightened, but Captain, I think you had a gun when first I seen you this morning: what have you done with her. I threw her away, says the Captain. A bad mark in an officer, says my father. Do you think you could find her? says my father. I do not know, says the Captain. I have orders, says my father, to take your guns from you, and I trust they will be given to those that will make better use of them than you are likely to do.

My father took the captain with him to Cedar Point, where he had started him in the morning, and took his track. In about one hundred yards they found his gun, and a little farther on they found his shotpouch. The cows were eating it, for at this time a good cow was the price of a bushel of alum salt and the people could not afford to give their cattle salt. They would eat every thing that would come in their way. My father picked up the bullets and some other little trinkets. He found twenty-two pewter bullets. Such was the urgency of the times that he had taken the little pewter he had on his shelf to make bullets to kill his neighbours.

This evening my father sent the prisoners to Miner's fort with the guard, all but one, that was D. F., and concluded to go to the house of J. S. and stay all night. With the family of J. S. was the Tory Justice, and [he] had administered the oath to more than one hundred men. He had not yet been taken, and his cattle [he] had driven away that day. J. S. was the uncle of D. F. and D. F. had insisted that my father would suffer him to go home and sleep that night with his wife. For, says he, I will probably be hanged, and this may be the last time I shall ever see her.

My father told him, I hope none of you will be hanged, that you will all be pardoned for your offences and yet become good citizens, but I will let you go and stay with your wife tonight, but you must certainly be at your uncle's early in the morning. Don't try to make your escape, for you cannot hide yourself in these woods but what I can find you, and you will

probably see your uncle J. S., and if you do, tell him to come
home and give himself up to me, that I will treat him as well
as the nature of the case will admit of, and he let him go.

My father was very much fatigued and went to bed, but
shortly afterwards J. S. came home and asked his wife if my
father was not in the house. She told him he was. He called
my father to get up. My father did so. The old man was as
sociable as the times would admit of. He says to his wife, The
Whigs have driven off my cattle. Yes, they have driven off my
sheep. Yes, they have destroyed my bees. Yes, they have
taken my stallion. Yes, well, God damn them. The taking [of]
this little steed horse hurt his feelings worse than all the rest.
The old man used to ride this little steed horse a-foxhunting,
and thought a great deal of him.

In the morning, D. F. was there according to promise.
When they was about to start, J. S. put on his shotpouch, his
tomahawk in his belt, and his gun on his shoulder, as if he
was going on a hunting expedition. My father says, Old man,
this will not do, as you are charged with a very serious offence, and I am about to deliver you over to the civil authority
that you may be tried for this offence. I do not wish to trat
you with any unnecessary harshness, but you must give your
gun to me. He did, but with apparent reluctance.

My father took them to the fort. It was customary with the
Whig party, when any of the Tories were brought in, to raise
a great yell and fire their guns. When my father came in with
the Tory Justice of the Peace, they were preparing to give the
usual salute, but my father prevailed on them to dispense
with it for this time. The officers joined a circle round him for
examination. The old man told his story. Now this is true,
said the old man, if God [were] sitting here with us. The
Justice of the Peace that Colonel Gaddis had brought with
him (whose name I have forgotten) told the old man that God
was everywhere present, that he knew all our actions and our
most secret thoughts.

CATCHING TORIES

In one of these tours catching Tories, my father had with him an Irishman of the name of James Milligan, a very warm Whig. They discovered four or five Tories standing close together apparently in deep consultation. They knew nothing of my father's party. James Milligan says with a low voice, I'll first take shot at the camp. As he presented his rifle, my father took hold of the cock of his gun or blood would have been shed.

The manner of examining Tories [was] as follows: When a man was brought in on suspicion of Toryism, he was asked by the proper officers, Have you ever taken the oath of allegiance to the State? If he said he had not, the next question was, Have you any objection to take it? If he said he had no objection, the oath was administered and the following certificate given him:

> I do hereby certify that David Wright hath taken and subscribed the Oath of Allegiance and fidelity as directed by an Act of the General Assembly of this State, intitled An Act to Oblige the Free Male Inhabitants of This State Above a Certain Age to Give Assurance of Allegiance to the Same and For Other Purposes. Witness my hand and seal [the] twenty-seventh day of August 1777.
>
> [signed] Thomas Gaddis

The Tories, when the foregoing questions were put to them, (with one exception) they refused to take it. They said they had recently taken an oath to the King and could not take both, and were instantly put into confinement. The foregoing exception was E. W. He had lived in one of my father's cabins shortly before. When asked if he had taken the oath of allegiance to the state, he said he had not. When asked if he had any objections to take it, he said he had none, and the oath was administered and a certificate give him. He told the court, if you have no more business with me, I wish to go to my cabin (he lived in the fort. I feel very unwell. He was dismissed -- send the next man. It was thought it was J. R.

He refused to take the oath to the State and acknowledged he had the foregoing Sunday taken the oath to the King, and he could not take both. The following questions were then put to J. R. Who administered the oath to you? J. S. was there. Any other persons took that oath on the same day? Yes, there was twenty-seven others. Do you know any of their names? Yes. Please to state them. The first name he mentioned was E. W. Is this the same E. W. that has just now taken the oath of allegiance to the State? Yes. Why, the villain ought to be hanged, says Col. Gaddis, No wonder he was sick!

These words were spoken rather thoughtlessly by Col. Gaddis, but was taken earnest by many of the Whig party. They ran to the cabin of poor little E. W. and pulled him out of bed, and a man brought a new cord with which man had never before been hanged, and put one end round the neck of E. W. and took him on a point a short distance above the fort, where there was a white limb that came square out from the body of the tree about ten feet from the ground. The other end of the rope was thrown over this limb and poor E. W. suspended between Heaven and earth for a short time, his wife screaming and pulling him down by the feet.

At this critical moment, my father and another strong man made their way into the crowd and cut the rope and saved the life of this poor little ignorant chair-maker, for that was his trade. However, he lay dead for some time. He had sworn to the King and he had sworn to the State, and he would have been of no use to either. It would have been a useless waste of human life to put to death such a poor creature. However, my father met with him some months after the Tory affair was over at some gathering of the people, I have forgot on what occasion. He came to my father and gave him his

hand. How do you do, Mr. Crawford. You have the advantage
of me, says my father, I don't know you. Why, is it possible
you don't know me -- my name is E. W. Oh, says my father, I
know you now. I saved your life at Miner's fort when you were
half hanged. Such was my father. He was willing to make fun
of this poor fellow now, although but a few months before he
had saved his life at the risk of his own.

The most dangerous of those men were sent to Williams-
burgh, Virginia, in irons, to the number of sixteen or eighteen, under the direction of the Revd. John Corbly, who was
at that time a Justice of The Peace for the State of Virginia.
He marched them on by slow marches, preaching and praying all the way, and did not arrive till a day or two after the
proper time. This was thought by many an intentional thing
on the part of Mr. Corbly, and proceeded from a principle of
humanity, as he wished no man's life to be taken for a mistaken policy. They were all pardoned and took the oath of
allegiance to the State and returned to their families.

DESERTERS

There was another class of them, as soon as they were
apprehended as Tories, enlisted and joined the army, and
shortly afterwards deserted. I have a recollection of twelve of
[the] last class. They had to play Bo-peep, for the Whigs of
that day would no more give quarters to a deserter than to a
Tory. I remember three of them -- A. F., W., and D. They had
been Tories. They had enlisted to save their necks from the
rope and deserted. They dare not stay in the settlement,
hence they started to the wood to hunt, about twenty-five
miles from their former place of residence on the headwaters
of Indian Creek. They found a waste cabin and made it their
hunting camp.

They had been there but a short time till they were discovered by the Indians. This cabin had no floor but the earth, a
fire in one end, and a few broad stones for a back wall. These
men was sleeping in their blankets before the fire. [The fire]

was then nearly burned out and the cabin in the dark. The Indians, in order to have a light, split a wiping stick, greased it with deer tallow, and put it in through the logs of the cabin and through the back wall into the fire. This soon catched and made a good light, on which they commenced killing the men.

One of the Indians tomahawked A. F. and dragged him out of the cabin and left him for dead, and returned into the cabin to assist in killing the other two men. When this was going on, A. F. came a little to himself and made his escape and came to Miner's fort before daylight, a distance of more than twenty miles. He was in a most shocking condition, without hat or shoes, and badly wounded. In this sad condition he refused to give any satisfactory account of himself or his companions.

The people of the fort sent for my father, as was usual in all such cases. The distance was seven miles. I was at the time five years old, and was at that time afflicted with a complaint called the shingles and supposed to be in a dangerous way. However, my father left me and went to see the wounded Tory and deserter. I remember my mother took me to Margaret McDowell, the only physician we had in the country at that time. She daubed me over with black cat's blood -- I suppose white cat's blood would have had the same effect. However, I got well.

But to return to the wounded Tory. When my father came to him, he says, A., I suppose you and your companions, if they are living, are under an oath of secrecy to each other, as you and them were acting in defiance of the laws. We think your companions are most likely killed, and we wish to find them and bury them. We do not wish you to violate your oath, if you are under any to them. We think you are sufficiently punished for all the crimes you have committed. At this poor A. J. was melted into tears and gave them some directions where to find his companions, which on the fourth day in the afternoon they found and buried.

They were both lying dead in the cabin. Their faithful dog was lying by them. The Indians had not killed him. There was more than half a bushel of men's blood in a low place in the earthen floor. Yet the dog had not lapped any of it, though the poor creature had been four days without eating.

I shall now give an account of another Tory deserter of the name of T. H. He was a perfect limb of the devil. He [en]listed to save his neck from the halter, as did many others. He deserted, was taken and pardoned, deserted a second time, was taken and pardoned, deserted a third time, was taken and shot at Fort Pitt. This man robbed and plundered wherever he went in the Winter of 1777. He kept the neighborhood of my father in continual alarm. His hopes were that, as the event of our struggle with Great Britain was very doubtful at that time, they dare not shoot him.

He had at one time scared away the people from the sugar camps, and broke their potmetal. He had a wife and family living two and a half miles from my father. My father had threatened that if he could get sight of him, that he would take him or die in the attempt.

One Richard Hall, a lad of about seventeen years of age, was out hunting in the snow. He came on the track of T. H. He followed him until T. H. killed a deer, and Hall made all speed to take him before he could load his gun. But T. H. was too quick for him. He was loaded before Hall came up, and kept him off, but they held a considerable conversation at a distance. T. H. told him, I understand Bill Crawford says he will take me at the risk of his life, but tell him, by God, if he attempts it, I will take his life. They parted.

He would sometimes come to his wife in the night, and be off before day. She lived in [the] kitchen of her brother-in-law, of the name of Vantress, who was a Whig. One night he came and his brother-in-law found it out. He came to my father (I remember the night perfectly). My father collected five or six of his Whig neighbours. They came to the place as soon as possible. They took a heavy rail from the fence and put it [on] four or five of their shoulders, and came against the door with the end of the rail with all their force, and knocked off a plank and sprang in and took him -- he was lying in bed with his wife before the fire -- and as soon as it was day they sent him under guard to Fort Pitt, where he was kept in the guardhouse for several months, when him and two others were shot.

He continued to brave them out till one of the others were shot, and he then begged the officers, For God's sake to let him live for one hour, but this was not granted. He was shot instantly. When the news arrived of his death in my father's fort, all the women and children shed tears except his son, a boy of about ten years of age. He was not the least affected.

The following statement of the misfortune of one of the Tory's families I will give as I heard it current at the time, without vouching for its truth.

The British agents had stated to their Tory friends that an arrangement had been made with the Indians, that if the Tories would have a white flag at their houses, the Indians would respect the flag and not destroy them. In consequence of this, a man by the name of C. shortly after the Tories were quelled left Gerard's fort and went to his plantation four miles from the fort, and had his white flag displayed, when the Indians came and killed him and his wife and four children. This was the first mischief after the Tory affair.

It was then seen that the Indians were no respecters of persons, so that the bulwark of our religion (as John Randolph says) would give them a half joe for every scalp. It was a matter of indifferency to them whether that scalp came off the head of a Whig or a Tory. When we consider the honest relation of the old honest W. that Gen. Burgoyne was to send a part of his army to take Fort Pitt on a certain day, and that the Indians were to take Wheeling on the same day, and when we consider that the Indians did attack Wheeling on that very day [September 1, 1777], the foregoing story appears very reasonable.

TORIES AND FEDERALISTS

I have said in this narrative that I have more sympathy for the Tories of 1777 than the party in opposition to the measures of Government before and at the time of the late war -- I will not call them the Federalists for they do not deserve the name, for all their measures tended to embarrass the Federal Government and encourage the Government of Great Britain to continue her spoilations of our commerce. At one time they charged Mister Jefferson with wishing to embroil us in a war with England. At a subsequent period they branded him as a coward and that he was afraid to go to war.

When war appeared inevitable, they opposed every measure of preparation. When war was declared, they abused the party in power for going to war without being prepared. One favourite argument was a division of the states: this they ,ore than hinted on the floor of Congress. When our difference with England was to all appearance adjusted, they extolled Mr. Madison to the skies and declared that when Mr. Jefferson was in office, he could at any time have brought about an adjustment of our differences on the same terms, but that Mr. Jefferson was hostile to England but subservient to the interest of France. But in a short time we receive the account that Great Britain had disavowed the acts of her minister, Mr. Erskine. Then the same party abused Mr. Madison for treating with Mr. Erskine at all, and alleged that Mr. Madison knew at the time that Mr. Erskine had no sufficient powers.

I was at Pittsburgh in the Summer of 1814 when the express arrived without any mail, and stated that the City of Washington was on fire, that the enemy had taken and burnt it. The man had only seen the fire at a distance and expected the whole city was destroyed. He was only three days from the city. I was a stranger, having only a short acquaintance with the tavern keeper with whom I had formerly put up. His name was G. M. I met him on the pavement near his house. Mr. G. M., have you heard this dreadful calamity? Yes, I hope it will have a good effect. I think it will unite the parties. I hope not, says Mr. G. M. Is it possible you would allow the enemy to overrun the country? I would rather come under the British Government than be governed by a God damned mob, says Mr. G. M.

I was at this time acting under a commission from the Governor of Pennsylvania [Simon Snyder -- JCL] to survey and take the fall of the ripples in the Monongahela River. Had this not been the case, I should probably have measured the length of Mr. G. M. on the pavement. I have since learned that Mr. G. M. has a number of brothers all well disposed to the Government, that he was the only black sheep in the flock.

If I was asked, did the leaders of the opposition to the measures of Government wish to destroy it, I answer, No, all that they wished was to render the present men in power unpopular that they might get their places. But still I am firmly of the opinion that the conduct of the opposition produced the last war, and they are in great measure chargeable with all the blood of the nation that [was] shed in defence of our rights. Great Britain was as much deceived, as this country was injured, by the opposition party, for they expected that in case of war, the New England states would separate themselves from the Union. This never was intended by any man of sense, for the middle and southern states can do better without the New England states, than the New England states can do without them.

I will now turn to the Tories of [the] western part of Pennsylvania of 1777. Their conduct no man can justify and their ignorance is their best excuse. They had emigrated from the east of the mountains because they were poor and unable to purchase land there. Here they had taken up land and had made small improvements on which they were barely enabled to raise their bread. With a very few exceptions, they were very ignorant. The thought of losing their lands and improvements were dreadful to them. It was their all. As Smith of Dellaway had deluded A. J., A. J. in my opinion deluded the rest.

A. J. had more wealth than any other man in his neighborhood. He was good to the poor, and further, he was better informed than most men of that day and place of universal ignorance, and beside all this (except the Tory affair) was ever considered an honest man. The reader may see by the confession of J. R. that twenty-seven had taken the oath on the Sunday previous to their detection, and had they been permitted to go on for three or four weeks longer, their numbers would have been such as to look down all opposition, at least till assistance could have come from over the mountain.

TORIES AND TORY OATHS

When I reflect on the situation of North Carolina about three years afterwards, where the Whigs hanging the Tories and the Tories hanging the Whigs was the work of almost every day for many months, [I remark] that the Tories were quelled in this country with the loss of but one life in the hands of the Whigs, and that was made out to be accident. This Tory was of the name of H [Hinkson -- JCL]. He was in irons and they were bringing him over Cheat River near the forks in a canoe. He fell out near the shore. He sunk and came up several times, and it was said he called for help.

Unfortunately, the Whig party had a bottle of whiskey at this time and were handing it round amongst them, drinking health to the States, to the success of General Washington and the Army of the United States, etc. till poor H. sunk to rise no more. Col. M. [Zackwell Morgan -- JCL] had the command of the Whig party. He was arrested and tried, but acquitted. The grave of poor H. is paled [?] exactly in the forks of Cheat and Monongahela, as a monument of the folly of men on publick business making too free with the bottle.

I have never been able to get hold of the form of the Tory oath, for they had two kinds, as I understood at the time from my father and others. The first was to keep secret whatever might be revealed to them hereafter. The second was to be true to the King. This came out in the examination of one of my father's neighbours by the name of R. I. He refused to take the oath of allegiance to the State. He was asked by Col. Gaddis if he had taken the oaths to the King. He said he had taken a kind of plantation oath. What do you mean by a plantation oath? says Col. G. It was to keep secret whatever they would tell me, says R. I.

After the war had come to a close, most of the Tories felt very unhappy. Most of them sold their possessions and went to other parts of the United States, and some of them went to Canady. But some few remained among us. They were generally peaceable the balance of their lives. There is very few (if any) of them now living. There are some of their descendants among us, as worthy men as any in our country, and as much attached to our form of Government as any other men living.

Military Reminiscences of Captain Henry Jolly (1757-1842) Covering the Years from 1776 to 1794

Henry Jolly, the author of the following, was born in Chester County (Pennsylvania), on the 20th day of December, 1757. In the tenth year of his age, his father moved his family to York County, out of the South Mountain where he resided until the year 1770 or 1771, when he moved west of the mountain and located in the vicinity of Catfish Camp (now Washington, Pennsylvania). There he resided at the commencement of our difficulties with Britain.

O N THE 15TH DAY of March, in the year 1776, myself and an older brother enlisted into the Pennsylvania State service, and was stationed at the Kittaning (Kittaningan) on the Allegheny River, until some time in the month of August, when we enlisted into the 8th Regiment of the Pennsylvania Line, on the Continental Establishment, and said regiment until used was stationary on the Kittangan, until the month of December, when orders came to march to headquarters in Jersey.

CAMPAIGNING IN THE JERSEYS

We kept our Christmas in Bedford, and marched out of Carlisle, Pennsylvania, on the morning of the 1st day of January, 1777 (if I am not mistaken), by the way of little York and Lancaster, to Philadelphia, then on board of shallops to Trenton, then by the way of Prince-Town and Somerset, to Quibbletown, immediately on the lines, and the very next morning I had the pleasure of drawing a bead on a British red coat, but without the desired effect. The distance was too great.

Colonel Richard Butler took command of the Regiment at that post, when everything began to wear a different aspect, the change in us for the better. We performed hard duty at said post, until about the 1st of March, when we moved to Bound-Brook, that post commanded by General Lincoln. There we had frequent skirmishing with the enemy, until the morning of the 13th of April, when the British took the post with about 33 prisoners, of whom my brother was one. I never saw him afterward. He died a prisoner in New York.

Some short time after that, about 100 men were detached from the said Regiment and attached to a Rifle Regiment commanded by Colonel Daniel Morgan, and Van Swearingen our Captain. Our officers told us that we were thirteen times engaged with the enemy in eleven days. This was in Somerset County, Jersey, in June 1777. The British soon after embarked and put to sea. General Washington marched to Germantown and encamped. I suppose it was deemed a proper place to watch the landing of the enemy.

THE SARATOGA CAMPAIGN

I think it was about the 1st of August that the Rifle Regiment left the grand army in Germantown common and went on the Northern Campaign. We marched by way of Trenton, Princetown, Somerset, and to Kingsbury on the river, thence on board of shallops to Albany. We landed immediately, formed in the street, and marched up into the Mohawk River, a little above the falls, where we encamped a few days. Then we crossed the river and joined the main army, commanded by General Gates, and flanked the said army to Stillwater.

There the army fortified, and waited the approach of the enemy, which happened on the 19th of September, and after a hard-fought battle of nearly five hours, the darkness of the night put an end to the engagement, and the two armies remained stationary, until the 7th of October, when the British came out and offered battle. At the discharge of their first cannon, up went the bloody flag in our camp, I think 50 or 60 feet high (the only time that I have ever seen the bloody flag hoisted). We then marched out. Colonel Morgan was ordered to an elevated piece of ground covered with timber. General Arnold moved on with his Brave Yankees, and attacked the British Grenadiers, and drove them from their cannon. Colonel Morgan and his riflemen descended like a torrent upon the right wing of the British Army, and though I believe I have been at least fifteen times engaged with the enemy, I have never seen so great a carnage, in so short a time, by the same number of men engaged.

The poor Germans suffered indeed. When the Germans gave way, we charged the right wing of the British Grenadiers, who also fled, leaving their Major Acland wounded, who fell into our hands a prisoner. We pursued them to their breastwork, and after a few minutes heavy firing from their cannon, we entered their breastwork. I was within a few paces of General Arnold when he fell, his leg broken and his horse killed.

It has ever been my opinion that if the darkness of night had not put an end to the engagement, the British Army would have been compelled to surrender at mercy. But they stole a night march a few days after, and retreated to Saratoga, fortified, and defended themselves as well as they could until the 17th of October, when they surrendered the whole army prisoners of war.

THE CAMPAIGN AROUND PHILADELPHIA

Colonel Morgan, the next day after the surrender, marched for headquarters in Pennsylvania, headquarters about fourteen or fifteen miles from Philadelphia. Some few days after our arrival at headquarters, a part of the Rifle Regiment was detached into Jersey, under the command of Lieutenant-Colonel Richard Butler, of which I was one. There we formed a junction with part of the Virginia troops, commanded by General La Fayette (I believe his first command, and see his biography). We were engaged three days in succession. On the third day the British crossed the Delaware into Pennsylvania. The next day we left the Jerseys for Pennsylvania, crossed the Delaware a little below Burlington, and joined the Army at Whitemarsh.

The British were under march in full force to offer battle to General Washington. The riflemen went out, attacked the front of the right wing, and a very hard engagement took place, and we had eighteen men killed. They gave us a cross-fire, and sixteen men fell, we believed all dead. I was left almost alone. Colonel Morgan was, I believe, about twenty yards to my left hand, and I think there was not more than one soldier left standing between us. A very tall redhaired sergeant fell against me. I was severely wounded in my clothes, but the flesh and bones escaped.

The British that night retreated to Philadelphia, and General Washington went into winter quarters at Valley Forge, and the riflemen to hard duty on the lines. The above engagement took place on the 7th of December, 1777, I believe on Monday. I assisted in the capture of the Dragoons: they were in an impassable bog, and were made prisoners without firing a gun. I also assisted at the taking of five teams, each team five horses, well harnassed, my share of the prize something over 100 pounds (Pennsylvania currency).

FORT McINTOSH AND FORT LAURENS

Around the 1st of June 1778, Swearingen's company rejoined the 8th Regiment of the Pennsylvania Line, and marched for Pittsburgh. From Carlisle a part of the Regiment made an excursion up the east branch of the Susquehanna, but without any good effect. From Carlisle we took up the line of march to Pittsburgh, then to Fort McIntosh, which was on the way of building. General McIntosh moved the Army onto the Tuscarawas fork of Big Muskingum, and erected Fort Laurens on the west bank. In a day or two after, the Army arrived there.

Three companies of Light Infantry were detached to Fort McIntosh for the purpose of escorting provision to the new fort, to wit, one company of Militia, one of Virginia, one of Pennsylvania, of which I was one, and after tarrying perhaps a week at Fort McIntosh, the pack horses were loaded and set out again for the new fort, and on Sandy Creek we met the army returning, and our militia company returned with them, leaving two companies to escort the provisions to the fort. However, we went on and delivered the flour, etc., and the Virginia company remained in the fort, leaving the Pennsylvania company to guard about thirty horses, etc. We were commanded by a lieutenant we considered a poor devil.

However, we all arrived safe to Fort McIntosh, I believe on the 21st of December. We had snow and very cold weather, a deep snow, less than half rations, etc. I had then to perform garrison duty, which to me was very disagreeable, but as Providence ordered, I in a few days obtained the privilege of taking a passage on a boat to the mouth of Muddy Creek, from Fort McIntosh perhaps 100 miles by water. I was detained there some weeks, in consequence of the ice in the river, where I lived deliciously, but got back to Fort McIntosh just as the General was preparing his second trip to Fort Laurens.

The provision at that time was carried mostly by volunteers with pampered horses, not inured to firing, and the garrison, at the approach of relief, fired a feu de joy, which started the horses, and a great part of the provision was lost. It was in the dark of the evening. I saw the flour flying like snow drifting, and many horses were out all night. Colonel

Gibson returned with General McIntosh, and Major Vernon was left in command of the garrison, and we returned all safe to Fort McIntosh. So much for the General's last tour to Fort Laurens.

Soon after our return to Fort McIntosh, our Regimental headquarters moved to Pittsburgh. In the Spring of the next year (1779), we descended the Ohio from Pittsburgh to the Mingo Bottoms, within three boats loaded with provision, guarded by two companies of light infantry, commanded by Captain Beall, a clever little man but poor military officer, who soon arrived on the opposite shore from the mouth of Cross Creek. We marched to Fort Laurens with the provision.

THE RESCUE OF THE HENRY CHILDREN

In the Spring of the year 1779, Captain Samuel Brady, with a party of veterans from the 8th Regiment of Pennsylvania, left Pittsburgh for the purposes of scouting on the frontier between Hannas-town (Greensburgh), Ligonier, and the Allegheny River. After traversing for some time the wilds between the frontier and the said river, he came on the trail of a party of Indians, going from the frontier settlement.

He pursued with all possible speed, until night caused them to lie down until daybreak, when they resumed their pursuit, but did not go far until they heard the sound of a tomahawk, and rightly supposed it to be the Indians preparing to cross the river. He immediately formed his men into a curve, and came very near them undiscovered, and then charged rapidly, leaving the Indians no possible chance of escape, but by swimming the river, which they attempted to do.

But the fire was so close and so well directed that there was not one seen to reach the opposite shore. One scalp only was taken, three children, two horses, and considerable other plunder retaken. The writer was in camp in the commons of Pittsburgh when Brady and his party returned with the trophies of their victory. He was also well acquainted with Captain Brady, and every man on that command.

BRADY'S INDIANS

In the months of August and September, in the year 1779, the 8th Regiment of Pennsylvania was reduced by the dismissing of about 200 soldiers, at least 100 of them having served with Morgan in the year 1777, which left the balance of the Regiment a compound of invalids, British deserters, etc. However, Captain Brady, out of this heterogeneous mass (his own words) selected a party painted and dressed like Indian warriors, and they went, and after travelling some days, they came in sight of an Indian village, where they lay concealed for some time, looking at the Indians, sporting by horse-racing.

While lying there, hoping to get some advantage of the Indians, three squaws came upon them, but believing Brady and his party to be Indians, made no attempt to escape, and were made prisoners. Some were for killing them on the spot; others were for taking them prisoners. Brady preferred the latter, and off they travelled for the Ohio River, and within about 12 or 14 miles of Fort McIntosh, they met a small party of Indians, with a female prisoner taken on the frontier of Washington County, Pennsylvania.

The two parties came together very close before they discovered each other. Brady instantly shot one. The rest fled, but when he looked around for his party, they had fled also. He was then left with his white female captive. With difficulty they reached Fort McIntosh that night. He returned with a small party the next day, and took the Indian's scalp and gun. His party got safe to Pittsburgh. This was in the Spring or Summer of 1780.

These notes are founded on fact, and are worth a great many Cuyahoga stories, which have no foundation in truth. I do not believe Captain Brady ever caught a beaver in his life.

I will make some references: Alexander Mitchell near Wheeling, Captain George Case near Wellsburgh, Captain John Buskirk, Newark, Ohio. These gentlemen all served with Captain Brady as spies, etc.

KILLBUCK AND THE TALL PINE

In the month of April, in the year 1781, Colonel Daniel Brodhead formed an expedition against the Indians residing at Coshocton, and for that purpose, appointed his general rendezvous at the mouth of Wheeling, where the Militia and Volunteers assembled, while he ascended the Ohio with the regular troops from Pittsburgh.

He had one old friendly Indian with him as a guide, and on his way, he found another Indian by the name of Killbuck, whom he took on board and kept him in close confinement, lest he should convey intelligence to the hostile Indians. And when they arrived at Wheeling, the old guide thinking the guard house would be a safe and comfortable place to lodge, went in with the prisoner, but the volunteers made up a small party (Lewis Wetzel one) and appointed a James Clark, on account of his great strength, to seize the sentinel, which he did, and held him fast, until Wetzel and three or four more had finished Killbuck.

They then made their escape to the Militia Camp. Wetzel went the campaign and returned safe. The writer was well acquainted with the two Indians. He had been in the woods with both of them. He formed a favorable opinion of the old guide (Scare The World, he called himself), but had no confidence in the young man's friendship.

Some days after the return of the troops to Wheeling, a young man by the name of Mills, who had served on the campaign, solicited Wetzel to go with him in quest of his horse that he had left a few miles from the river. Wetzel was always ready, crossed the river, and in travelling a short distance, they met a party of Indians. Wetzel shot and killed one. They returned the fire and shot and killed Mills, and Wetzel made toward the Ohio, at the same time turning up his powder horn to the muzzle of the gun, and one cant of the horn put in a full charge. Then dropping in one of his smallest bullets, his gun was charged. The bullets he carried in his mouth.

But he found they were flanking him on both sides, leaving him no possible chance of escape, but by making the best of his way to the river cliffs. But he found himself so closely pursued that he felt an Indian touch him two or three times, but did not get hold of him. He then sprung to one side, and so nigh was the Indian to him that when he fired, he had hold of his gun.

However, he made out to break his thigh. He then escaped by a miraculous leap over a cliff of rocks, and the Indians give over the chase, and he made good his retreat to Wheeling Fort.

It has been proved past a doubt that Wetzel at that time killed two Indians. When the party returned to their town, two of them were missing, and great was the lamentation of the Indians at the loss of The Tall Pine, a highly esteemed young Shawanese, whose thigh Wetzel no doubt broke. It is a fact that we never had a more correct account of that transaction than from the Indians themselves, through the medium of a number of persons who were prisoners with the Indians at the time. They described his leap, and his flying over the cliffs they charged to the interposition of the Great Spirit.

The Tall Pine certainly did not expect that Wetzel's gun was loaded, or he would not have pursued him so close, and it is accident the Indians' guns were all empty, or they would have fired at him after his leap, for he run a considerable distance in view of them.

It was common in them times for riflemen to carry two sizes of a bullet, one size suited to the calibre of the gun, the other a size less but only to be used in cases of emergency. General Morgan used to say such charges would do for close fighting, and so it happened with Wetzel and The Tall Pine.

THE WETZEL FAMILY

Captain John Wetzel was one of the first settlers on the frontiers of Virginia. His residence was on Wheeling, about nine or ten miles from the mouth of Big Graves Creek. When the Indians began to commit depradations on the frontiers, he and his family were much exposed to their ravages. He had five sons, Martin, George, Lewis, Jacob, and John.

Martin was taken prisoner and was with the Indians about two years. How he effected his escape the writer has forgot. Lewis and Jacob were taken prisoners when very young, Lewis at the same time slightly wounded. There was but two Indians, so that each one had a prisoner. Jacob has often said, that the one who had him treated him friendly. However, after crossing the Ohio and travelling a few miles, night came on, and the prisoners had to be tied. When the Indian was tying Jacob, he exclaimed, "Too tight. It hurts." He slacked it a little. He again exclaimed, "Too tight. It hurts." He again slacked a little, and down they lay, and the Indians were soon fast asleep. Jacob easily extricated himself and very soon unshackled his brother, and with all possible speed they retraced their steps back again to the Ohio. Thus, by the lenity of a savage, two prisoners effected their escape.

Some time after this, the old man, with three or four of his sons, ascending the Ohio near Muskingum Island (Meigs Island), was fired upon by a party of Indians on the shore, and George mortally wounded. He expired in a short time, and was buried on the upper point of Pursell Island, that is, the first island below Sistersville.

Jacob was very serviceable on the frontier as a spy. He was with Captain Brady on many hazardous adventures, and it is a fact that he was by many thought to be at least equal to Brady. He was acknowledged to be the best woodsman on that line of frontier. He married soon after the close of the war, and was some years High Sheriff of Ohio County. He emigrated many years ago to Illinois.

Martin Wetzel resided immediately on the frontier. He was at no time (I believe) in actual service, but he held himself in readiness to turn out in every emergency, by which he rendered very essential service to this part of the frontier. He is probably at this time living on Wheeling, as the writer has never heard of his death or removal.

The captivity of John Wetzel and his liberation by Isaac Williams and Hamilton Karr, is long since published in *The American Friend.*

OTHER STORIES OF LEWIS WETZEL

I feel confident that I had knowledge of every transaction of Lewis Wetzel from the year 1780 until the close of the Indian War. His first achievement was killing young Killbuck in the guardhouse, killing The Tall Pine, etc., his adventure when the Indians killed his father, his wounding Indian Washington, and his escape from Fort Harmar. He also went a volunteer on a campaign from Kentucky, under the command (I believe) of Colonel Logan. Near about the close of the Indian War he went to New Orleans, and for some offence, or supposed offence, he was imprisoned and kept in close confinement for a considerable length of time.

But his friends interested themselves in his favor (your obedient servant for one) and sent on a petition to the Governor, praying him to liberate Lewis Wetzel from his confinement, which request was granted, and Wetzel once more at liberty. Mr. Colerick, editor of the first newspaper printed at Washington, drafted the petition, and a Daniel Moore of the same place took it to New Orleans. It was consigned to a person there who attended to it. Since that I know nothing of Lewis Wetzel.

I do expect that Wetzel's Dunkard story, and Brady's Cuyahoga leap, will have to descend to posterity as fact; but I must and do protest against it. There never was that man born or rifle made that could perform what is attributed to Wetzel.

I will observe that all Wetzel's services were voluntary. I never knew him to be under pay one hour of his life, but was ready in every emergency to turn out for the protection of the frontier settlements, whereas the Rangers were under pay, and the Spies had each one dollar per day, and many lazy devils joined the Rangers, for the purpose of receiving rations and lying about the fort, and it is said that some are receiving pensions.

In the year [1784], when I first became acquainted with the Bonnett family, they had two boys, one I think under five, and the other not more than three years old, so that all they can tell about the Wetzels must be from hearsay.

THE INDIAN CAMPAIGN OF 1781

Sometime in August in the year 1781, a large party of hostile Indians came to the Moravian town, on Big Muskingum, and encamped round the town, for the purpose of preventing the Moravians' conveying intelligence to the frontier settlements. But a crippled squaw was permitted to pass out, and conveyed the intelligence to Fort McIntosh, from there to Pittsburgh to Colonel Brodhead, Commandant of the Western Department, and from him to the different leading officers on the frontier.

Volunteers immediately turned out to the frontier forts. About twelve of us went from the vicinity of Washington, Pennsylvania, and went to Vanmeter's Fort. We arrived there in the evening, and on that day, a small party of Indians came in, and killed three or four hogs that Major McCulloch had in pen on his farm, took two or three horses, etc., crossed the Ohio above Wheeling, and were gone. The small party from Washington, concluding the danger was over for that time, returned to our home, but the next day we received intelligence that a large party of Indians had crossed the river at Boggs Island, three or four miles below the mouth of Wheeling.

We immediately collected and retraced our steps back to the frontier. The Indians when they crossed the river took up Middle Wheeling, until they came to Link's Blockhouse, which had been abandoned for some short time, but at that time there were three or four men in it. I am not able to name any of them to a certainty but Jacob Miller, but my impression is that old Philip Hupp on Duck Creek had one or two brothers killed there.

Miller was chief spokesman and made conditions for himself, or at least so the Indians construed it, and as soon as the door opened they killed all but Miller: him they saved. From there they went to the ridge dividing the waters of Wheeling and Buffalo Creek. Then, discovering two farms, and seeing people at each farm, they separated, so that they might surprise both at the same time. One farm belonged to William Hawkins, the other to Peak.

Just as they were preparing to make their descent, a party of about twenty volunteers on horseback (of which I was one) passed between them and the places they meant to attack. However, they rushed on, and how many they killed at Hawkins's I do not recollect, but they took Hawkins and his daughter prisoners (I will if strength permits before I close give an account of the miraculous escape of Mrs. Hawkins and her infant babe), and the two parties met at Peak's, from where they commenced their retreat toward the Ohio. Travelling a short distance, they halted, and tied three of the prisoners to saplings, and after talking to them a while, enquiring about the number of men that might be on the frontier, the answer not less than 150 men at that time between them and the Ohio, they then tomahawked the three tied prisoners, and started rapidly for the Ohio.

The three prisoners tomahawked were Hawkins, Link, Burnet. They had four other prisoners, to wit, Jacob Miller, Presley Peak, a Miss Hawkins, and Miss Walker. Miller that night made his escape and came to us next morning, and gave a full account of what the Indians had done, and they were at that time over the river, he thought about 70 or 80. We then went and buried the dead and returned to our homes. The Indians on their return carried off the whole of the Moravians, I believe, to Upper Sandusky, and after some time, finding that the Moravians had not the means of subsistence, the hostile Indians permitted a part of them to return to winter on their own potatoes, etc., particularly the invalid old men, women, and children.

This accounts for the great proportion of women and children that were murdered in the March following. The above named Jacob Miller has said in detached conversation that it was said 82 Moravians were killed, besides seven men who had some of the appearance of warriors. They did not mix with the Moravians, took no part in their devotions, but had a separate apartment for themselves.

When it was decided the Moravians must die, Miller and a few others tried to get out of hearing, but (alas, said he) "the death screams outwent us." This and much more I have heard from Jacob Miller, whose veracity I believe was never impeached by them that knew him.

Hawkins's house was built on a small branch of Buffaloe Creek, which made a high bluff bank, and when the Indians made their attack, Mrs. Hawkins snatched up her infant babe, and over the bluff and in the stream she went. The high bluff completely hid her from the Indians. She kept down the stream perhaps ten or fifteen rods, and then turned up another stream, keeping in the water lest she should be tracked. But she soon observed three Indians coming up the stream right after her. She squatted in the water, and they passed by.

She then left the stream and took the high ground. The three that passed by her met an old man, by the name of Walker. He was on horseback, and his Daughter, a young woman, on behind him. The Indians fired, killed the old man, and took his daughter and horse, and on their return, they again missed Mrs. Hawkins. She squatted in the weeds, and they passed her as before.

The distressful creature and her infant lay in the woods all night, under a heavy rain some part of the time. The next day, as we were returning to our homes, a man rode ahead, and turned off on some business etc., and was waiting at the road. When we came up, he told us of the woman in distress and requested assistance, which was readily granted. A man turned out and away they went to fetch the woman and her babe, and as he was going out, he told that she had seen a party, sun about two hours high yesterday.

"My God, Indians here about two hours ago!" and the whole party appeared panic struck in a moment, and off they went, the fastest horse I believe foremost. I think there was not less than twenty-five of the party, and only two remained to assist the distressed woman. Such were the heroes of Washington County; such were the men who murdered the Moravians; such were the men that Colonel Williamson mostly commanded.

Colonel Williamson was no doubt a brave man, but it, which rarely happens, was mixed with a degree of cruelty very unbecoming a soldier. I will observe that Colonel Williamson was not with the party that so shamefully ran away and left the distressed woman.

HENRY JOLLY'S RETURN TO THE FRONTIER

After I left the Revolutionary Army, I laid my sleeve round a lass, and she readily agreed to move with me to the frontier, which we did in the Spring of 1783. The Militia at that time was poorly organized. An old veteran, Captain Lewis Bonnett, had the command of the Wheeling company, and there being a vacancy for an ensign, at the request of the captain and unanimous approbation of the company, and I agreed to serve as ensign.

About the time the commission came to hand, our venerable Captain resigned, and I was unanimously chosen as his successor, and was in a short time after commissioned by the Governor of Virginia, as Captain of a company of Militia, of the County of Ohio. I held said commission until the adoption of our present constitution, when I again received from the Governor of Virginia a commission, which I held until the ratification of Jay's Treaty. When I was on the Tuscarawas in 1778 and 1779, I belonged to a select company of Infantry on the Continental Establishment.

I some years ago made some notes that was published by Mr. Prentiss, but a debility in my right hand prevented my writing more at that time: the hazardous adventure of Lewis Wetzel when the Indians killed his father, the massacre of the Simms Family at the mouth of Fish Creek, the wound and miraculous escape of Nathan Parr, the killing of part of a family by the name of Jolly on Wheeling and another in the Kirkwood blockhouse, etc.

As my name is made use of, I wish the truth to be told, and I believe there is no person in existence that has an equal chance with myself, to know the affairs of that frontier, that is, from 1783 to 1794.

In a mistake, I have stated that I moved to the frontiers of Virginia in 1783, but by looking over some old papers, I find that I came unto the frontier on the 10th of April 1784. Lewis Bonnette (the father of Major Lewis Bonnett) had shortly before been commissioned to the command of a frontier company. It was my fortune to become his near and very intimate neighbour. He was (I think) one of the best men I ever was acquainted with. He had all the courage that was necessary for a Caesar or Alexander, but for military tactics

he was entirely ignorant. He had a Lieutenant who was deficient in everything necessary to constitute a soldier.

Bonnett requested me to take the commission of ensign. I
told him I would not, but I would give him all the assistance
in my power as to the police of his company. He was then
rising fifty years of age, and resigned his uniform about the
year of 1786, and the company (I believe unanimously)
requested me to take command of it, which I agreed to do,
and shortly afterward received a Captain's commission,
which command I held until the ratification of Jay's Treaty.

THE STORY OF NATHAN PARR, 1784

On the 26th of September, 1784, Nathan Parr passed by
my cabin on Wheeling, a little before sunset. He was in a
great hurry to get there before dark. He had passed but a
short time when I heard the report of two rifles in quick
succession. My wife was returning from a visit, and hearing
the firing was much alarmed, and hurried home, and insisted
to go to the cornfield, about thirty rods. But before we
reached the field, Parr overtook us, saying, "I have just made
my escape from the Indians." I told my wife (we had no children) to go with Parr to Colonel Shepherd's, and I rode out to
notify the people that were living at their homes, in hopes
that the Indians would not be for war, after the peace with
England, but it was a vain hope.

Next morning, four or five went to the place where the
Indians fired at him, and old Captain Wetzel and myself
placing our feet in the Indian's tracks, and laying our guns to
the same tree, and taking aim at the incision of the Indian's
ball in an oak on the opposite side of the path, it appeared
that the Indian fired at his head, which could not have been
more than six or seven feet from the muzzle of his gun when
he fired.

They killed his horse, but took his flour. I marked on a
beech tree, at the place, Nathan's defeat, Sept. 26, 1784,

which was conspicuous for many a day. In our tour, we called at a block-house, where we feasted on potatoes and buttermilk, which was very acceptable at that time, and for which I tried to be thankful.

THE SIMMS FAMILY

In the month of April in the year 1785 or 1786, the Indians crossed the Ohio at or near the mouth of Fish Creek, and found a family by the name of Simms, to wit, one old man and one old woman, a young man, a young woman, and two lads perhaps about twelve or thirteen years of age. The old man and one of the lads were on the high bottom. The old man was grubbing sumac, and one of the lads cutting a log within a few rods of him. The young man, his sister, and the other boy were planting corn in the lower bottom.

The Indians separated, part to the higher, and part to the lower bottom. The three in the lower bottom were all taken prisoners. The other party killed the old man with a war mallet, and shot the boy. The two parties then met at the house, took the old woman a short distance, and killed her with the war mallet, which they left lying beside her.

The same day they took two mares and a colored boy, the property of a James McMechan. On that night the people of the Station sent a runner to the forks of Wheeling, and four men started on horseback, and was early at the Station, and with a few from the Fort went to the place, and found the mangled bodies of the persons, an awful sight indeed. The writer of this note has seen hundreds lying in the battlefield, but it did not hurt his feelings as much as it did to see that old man and woman, lying, their brains beat out, etc.

But when I view six of a family, three made prisoners, and that by savages -- when I contrast it with the Moravian massacre -- it dwindles almost to nothing. The three were taken to the Indian town, and the young man, Samuel, found a means to escape, mounted a Canadian pony, and retraced his steps to the Ohio. The young woman (it was said) got married to a Frenchman at Detroit. The lad, Thomas Simms, was with the Indians (I think) ten or eleven years. He then returned to the Ohio, and after some time married, and located himself in Newport, where he resided until some time in the winter of 1822, when he departed this life, leaving a widow and three children to deplore their loss. The character of Thomas Simms was that of a very honest man. So much for the Simms family. They cannot speak for themselves.

THE DEATH OF CAPTAIN JOHN WETZEL

Some time in the summer of 1787 (if the writer is not mistaken), old Captain John Wetzel, with Lewis and two others, one by the name of Andrews and the other by the name of Moore, were passing up the river in a canoe, and when they came to the mouth of Fish Creek, Lewis felt a fit of the ague coming on him, and proposed going by land the nigh way up to the Station. But the party in the canoe, when about a mile from the Fort, were hailed by a party of Indians, telling them to come to shore. [Captain] Wetzel answered, "By and by," and at the same time thrust the canoe farther into the current. The Indians fired and killed Wetzel and Moore. Andrews escaped by swimming to the opposite shore. Lewis Wetzel, lying at the back of the bottom, a considerable distance from the river, hearing the firing hasted to the river, but the Indians had taken the canoe and gone to the opposite shore.

He, fearful for the fate of a party of hunters that crossed the river the day before (two of them his own brothers), immediately took to the river and swam to the opposite shore, carrying his gun, which he held in his left hand, the muzzle and part of the barrel under water, and pressed against his left shoulder, the lock and breech clear above the water, so that the essential part of the gun was dry.

Having gained the shore, he found that the Indians went on the trail of the hunters. There was five hunters, and each

one a horse, so that they were easy trailed. Wetzel followed
the track at least five miles, broke a bush across the track,
and returned to the Station, and after taking a little refreshment walked fifteen miles to the writer of this note, and the
next day we were early at the Station with about nine or ten
men, and immediately crossed the river, and pursued on the
trail of the Indians and hunters a short distance past where
Wetzel broke the bush, and found that the Indians had
separated from the trail of the hunters, the hunters turning
into the waters of Sunfish Creek, and the Indians kept the
dividing ridge.

We followed their tracks perhaps two or three miles, and
found that they kept wide of the hunters, and Wetzel taken
very sick, at his request we returned. The hunters came in
the next day, all safe, their horses loaded with venison, which
was truly valuable at that time. We conjectured that the
Indians thought the hunters to be a scouting party, and
being equal in number, and being encumbered with three
heavy rifles, as trophies of their victory (for they took no
scalps), thought safest to avoid them, and make the best of
their way out of danger.

INDIAN WASHINGTON

Early in the summer of the year 1789 (if the writer is not
mistaken), Lewis Wetzel and Vachel Dickerson fired at and
wounded an Indian who called himself George Washington,
but being on horseback, he made his escape to Fort Harmar.
General Harmar instantaneously offered a proclamation,
offering a reward for taking and delivering the said offenders,
or either of them, at Fort Harmar, but the General's proclamation passed on the frontier as a thing merely to be laughed
at.

But Wetzel, in order to cut a high swell (as he called it),
went to Marietta, and sent his compliments to the General,
informing him that he was there, if he had any business with
him to come on. But in a short time he was visited by a

Lieutenant Hartshorne, with a party of soldiers, who took him prisoner to the Fort, handcuffed him, and put him in the guardhouse. How long he was confined the writer is not able to say, but after some time he discovered that the guard was kept with empty guns, depending entirely on their bayonets, and when he had occasion to go to the necessary (which was outside the fort), he was guarded by two soldiers with fixed bayonets. He had also, while in the guardhouse, found that he could extricate his hands, which he had several times done, but one evening, as it began to be dark, he made a trip to the necessary, escorted as usual. But when they came to the place, he bid them good-bye, and soon gained the woods. But his hands had swollen so that he could not get them clear of the handcuffs, and deeming it impossible to swim the river handcuffed, he took his lodging for the night under a log.

In the morning, he went to the river and made a signal, which being discovered in Virginia, William Clemens of Washington County, Pennsylvania (who was there in the trading order), brought him over. He said that the soldiers from the Fort, and he believed some Indians, in searching for him, divers times crossed the log under which he lay, and ultimately concluded that he had undertook to swim the river, and was drowned.

Such was the prevailing opinion, until he called over the next day, to inform the General where he was, and if he would come himself, or send Mr. Hartshorne, they might have the handcuffs, which were useless to him. Wetzel has told the writer of this note, that while he was in Fort Harmar, he underwent several examinations, and the officers treated him with great civility. He spoke of Major Doty as his peculiar friend.

ANOTHER STORY OF NATHAN PARR

In the month of June 1789 (if I am not mistaken), Nathan Parr went from his father's to hunt, saying that if he killed nothing, he would lodge that night at Graves Creek Station, but within about twelve miles of it he killed a deer, and returned home. And on the next morning (Sunday), he set out with a horse, to pack home his deer, but within a short distance of his deer, riding in the water mark of Little Graves Creek, he discovered four Indians, a little behind him.

He tried to start his horse, but being surrounded with drift, the horse could not move forward. The Indians fired and wounded him severely in one of his hips. He then dropped his gun, hopped from his horse, and made for the hill, and was (it appeared) very close pursued. The Indians then give out the chase, killed his horse, and went off. Parr, by travelling about two miles, came to Clark's blockhouse, and a runner was immediately sent up to his father's, about seven miles.

As I passed by old Mr. Parr's on my way to Meeting, I saw him sitting in his colored shirt and trousers, and bareheaded. I went to Meeting, and when the congregation was seated in a beautiful shade, and the preacher had commenced talking to the people, I cast a look toward home, and discovered Old Man Parr, on horseback almost full speed. I hastened to meet him, and called out, "Stephen, what's the matter?"

"Nathan is at Clark's blockhouse, wounded by the Indians." I spoke to the people, requesting a few volunteers. Six fine strong young men turned out, and went to the blockhouse where Parr lay, and by his directions went to the place where the Indians fired at him, found his horse dead, etc. We then returned to the blockhouse, and carried him on a litter to his father's (seven miles). In about twenty-four hours, they had Dr. Baird from Washington, Pennsylvania, to him, and I believe he did not walk for six months. He remained a cripple through life. He married and raised a numerous family. He was an early settler in Washington County, Ohio. Nathan Parr was an active volunteer partisan against the Indians, therefore lamented by some, the writer of this for one. He died some years ago in Granville.

STORIES OF CAPTAIN BRADY

I positively assert that Captain Brady did not reside in Chartiers, until the 8th Regiment of Pennsylvania was disbanded at the close of the Revolution, and then but a very short time. The whole story about the Cuyahoga expedition is so unmilitary that I feel confident Captain Brady would never have been guilty of so base conduct: first, dividing his men to follow two trails, his ordering his men to disperse, and everyone to take care of himself, his leaping the Cuyahoga, his wound, swimming the pond under water; then, making his way home to Chartiers, wounded and without any means to procure sustenance, is a romance and ought not to be told as fact. However, such is my opinion.

I believe I have told you about Captain Brady, killing an Indian, liberating a white female captive, his party running away to Pittsburgh, and their apology for so doing was that the Captain had told them to shift for themselves, and I am not able to suggest anything else that could give rise to the Cuyahoga story.

Captain Brady was a true friend to his country, an honest man, and a brave soldier. He was a distinguished Ensign under Colonel Morgan in the months of May and June 1777. He merited applause for his conduct as a Lieutenant in the battle of Brandywine and Germantown, then about twenty years of age. He was proverbial for a tender-hearted benevolent man, and it is my belief Brady would run almost any risk to relieve a fellow mortal if he saw them in distress. So much for my old friend, to whose memory I cannot refrain dropping the tear of gratitude.

IN THE 1790s

In the Spring of the year 1790 or 1791, a party of Indians crossed the Ohio. It was at the time the people were attending their sugar camps, and the writer of this note, on hearing that they had crossed the river, raised a party of volunteers for the purpose of interrupting them on their return. He posted a small party at Pipe Creek, perhaps seven or eight men, another at the mouth of Captina.

With the balance, he himself took post at the mouth of Sunfish. The Indians went up Middle Wheeling, and killed a Houston, an Edgar, and several others whose names are forgotten. How many of the Beham family was killed I am not able to say, but two boys (striplings) were taken prisoners, and as they went off, they burnt the writer's house, and travelled until they came to the summit of the river hill a little below Fish Creek, and a short distance above Sunfish.

They halted for some time as if waiting to cross the river in the dark, but a little before sundown, a large boat descending the river raised a general fire at a flock of turkeys on shore, which alarmed the Indians of danger, and they immediately tomahawked and scalped the two prisoners, leaving them for dead.

But one of them came to, and made his way to Graves Creek parts, about the second or third day after he was scalped. I saw his head dressed by a William Ward, who resided at Graves Creek at that time. I have once seen him after he began to ride about. He was much disfigured. I understood he died soon after.

I will observe that I was an ear and eye witness to the boats [that] were firing on the turkeys. I was on the Indian shore with six men besides myself, hearing the firing perhaps about thirty rods up the river. We started and soon found what it was. These were the guns that alarmed the Indians.

My impressions is that the Indians left a horse hid where they tomahawked the boys, and that the surviving one rode him to Graves Creek, the distance perhaps ten or twelve miles. I do not state these as facts. But if it should be deemed necessary, I refer to my very old and much respected friend, Elizabeth Tomlinson, and her son Joseph. They can probably recollect how he came to Graves Creek. More than that, they cannot know. He (the dead one) was buried at an old deadening, called McIntosh's Deadening. I attended his burying. Joseph Tomlinson no doubt knows the places, the distance from Graves Creek, etc.,

Captain Henry Jolly Reviews Withers - *Chronicles of Border Warfare*

The first edition of Alexander Withers, Chronicles of Border Warfare, *was published by Joseph Israel, in Clarksburg, Virgina [now West Virginia], in 1831. The author, Alexander Scott Withers (1792-1865), a cousin of Sir Walter Scott, attended Washington College (now Washington & Lee) and the law department of William & Mary College in Williamsburg, Virginia. He collected reminiscences and papers for his* Chronicles *during the 1820s, in Virginia, but removed to Missouri, before returning to western Virginia, where he lived out his days. He was second in the field, after the Rev. Joseph Doddridge, in publishing an account of the heroic age on the Upper Ohio.*

In a letter in 1838 to Dr. Samuel Hildreth, Henry Jolly, then in his 82nd year, reviewed Alexander Withers, Chronicles of Border Warfare. *We have here printed the passages from Withers, if Captain Jolly does not quote them in full: the quotations from Withers will be printed first, followed by the comments by Captain Jolly. It will be noted that the comments are frequently addressed to points that Withers omitted. In some cases, Lyman Draper commented on these points, and his notes are printed with the identifying initials LCD. The other notes are mine.*

W ITHERS RECORDS, ON pages 49-50, the following:

*In the year 1756 settlements were also made on
New River and on Holston. . . . Nearly contemporane-
ous with these establishments was that at Gallipolis,
on the northwestern bank of the Ohio, and below Point
Pleasant, at the mouth of the Great Kenhawa.*

From Captain Jolly:

Certainly Gallipolis was not settled in the year 1756 or
1757.

Withers, on pages 104-105:

*In the year 1774, the peace, which had subsisted
with but little violation since the treaty of 1765, received an interruption, which checked for a while the
emigration to the North West frontier; and involved its
infant settlements in a war with the Indians. This
result has been attributed to various causes. Some
have asserted that it had its origin in the murder of
some Indians on the Ohio river both above and below
Wheeling, in the spring of that year. Others suppose it
to have been produced by the instigation of British
emissaries, and the influence of Canadian traders.*

*That it was not caused by the murders at Captina,
and opposite the mouth of the Yellow creek, is fully
inferrible from the fact, that several Indians had been
previously murdered by the whites, in a period of the
most profound tranquillity, without having led to a
similar issue; or even given rise to any act of retaliation, on the part of the friends or countrymen of those,
who had been thus murdered.*

*At different periods of time, between the peace of
1765, and the renewal of hostilities in 1774, three
Indians were unprovokedly killed by John Ryan, on the*

*Ohio, Monongahela, and Cheat rivers. The first who
suffered from the unrestrained licentiousness of this
man, was an Indian of distinction in his tribe, and
known by the name of Capt. Peter; the other two were
private warriors. And but that Governor Dunmore, from
the representations made to him, was induced to offer
a reward for his apprehension, which caused him to
leave the country, Ryan would probably have continued to murder every Indian, with whom he should
chance to meet, wandering through the settlements.*

From Captain Jolly:

I must disagree with Mr. Withers, on pages 104-105. I was
then about sixteen years of age, but very well recollect what I
have seen then, and information that I have since obtained
from (I believe) good authority. In the Spring of the year 1775,
a party of Indians encamped on the northwest of the Ohio,
near the mouth of Yellow Creek. A party of whites, called
Greathouse's party, lay on the opposite side of the river. The
Indians came over to the white party -- I think five men, one
woman, and an infant baby.

The whites gave them rum, which three of them drank,
and in a short time became very drunk. The other two men,
and the women refused. The sober Indians were challenged
to shoot at a mark, to which they agreed, and as soon as they
emptied their guns, the whites shot them down.

The women attempted to escape by flight, but was also
shot down. She lived long enough, however, to beg mercy for
her babe, telling them that it was a-kin to themselves. They it
was had a man in the cabin prepared with tomahawk for the
purpose of killing the three drunk Indians, which was
immediately done. The party of men and women removed off
for the interior settlements, and they came to Catfish Camp
on the evening of the next day, where they tarried until the
next day. I very well recollect my mother, feeding and dress-
ing the babe, chirping to the little innocent, and it smiling.

However, they took it away, and talked of sending it to its supposed father, Colonel John, who was then for several years with Colonel George Gibson of Carlisle, Pennsylvania, who had been and was then a trader for several years amongst the Indians.

The remainder of the party, at the mouth of Yellow Creek, finding that their friends on the opposite side of the river, was massacred, they attempted to escape by descending the Ohio, and in order to avoid being discovered by the whites, passed on to the west side of Wheeling Island, and landed at Pipe Creek, a small stream that empties into the Ohio a few miles below Graves Creek, where they were overtaken by a Cresap with a party of men from Wheeling.

They took one Indian scalp, and had one white man badly wounded (Big Terrance). They, I believe, carried him in a litter from Wheeling to Redstone. I saw the party on the return from the victorious campaign. (That portion of the narrative which relates to Captain Cresap agrees with the evidence of Colonel Eben Zane, published in Mr. Withers.)

The Indians had for sometimes before thought themselves intruded upon by the Long Knife, as they called the Virginians at that time, and many of them were for war. However, they called a council, in which Logan acted a conspicuous part. He admitted their ground of complaint, but at the same time reminded them of some aggressions on the part of the Indians, and that by a war, they could but harass and distress the frontier settlements for a short time, that the Long Knives would come like the trees in the woods, and that ultimately, they would be drove from their good land that they now possessed.

He therefore strongly recommended peace. To him they all agreed, grounded the hatchet. Everything wore a tranquil appearance, when behold, in came the fugitives from Yellow Creek -- Logan's father, brother, and sister murdered. What is to be done now? Logan has lost three of his nearest and dearest relations: the consequence is that this same Logan, who a few days before was so pacific, raises the hatchet, with a declaration that he will not ground it, until he has taken ten for one, which I believe he completely fulfilled, by taking thirty scalps and prisoners in the summer of 1774.

The above has oft been told to me by sundry persons who was off at the Indian town, at the time of the council alluded to, and also when the remains of the party came in from Yellow Creek. Thomas Nicholson has told me the above, and much more. Another person (whose name I cannot recollect) told me that he was at the towns when the Yellow Creek Indians came in, that there was a very great lamentation in the place by all the Indians of that places. Some friendly Indian advised him to leave the Indian settlement, which he did.

Could any person of common rationality believe for a moment that the Indians came to Yellow Creek with hostile intentions, or that they had any suspicion of the whites? Having any hostile intentions against them, would five men have crossed the river, three of them in a short time dead drunk, the other two discharging their guns, putting themselves entirely at the mercy of the whites, or would they have brought over a squaw, with an infant papoose, if they had not reposed their confidence in the friendship of the whites. Every person who is acquainted with the Indians knows better, and it was the belief of the inhabitants who were capable of reasoning on the subject, that all the depradations committed on the frontier by Logan and his party, [were] as a retaliation, for the murder of Logan's friends at Yellow Creek. I mean all the depradations committed in the year 1774. It was well known that Michael Cresap had no hand in the Massacre of Yellow Creek.

Withers, on page 173:

In the spring of 1778, General McIntosh, with the regulars and some militiamen, attached to his com-

mand, descended the Ohio river from Fort Pitt, to the mouth of Big Beaver -- a creek discharging itself into that river from the north-west. . . . Fort McIntosh was accordingly erected here, and garrisoned; a six pound-er mounted for its defence.

From Captain Jolly:

Fort McIntosh built in the summer and fall of 1778, but no cannon until (I think) near the last of September, when the eight pounders -- one was mounted in each bastion, and two in the centre of the Fort (see page 173 [of Withers]).

Withers, on page 191:

Early in January [1779], a considerable body of savages approached Fort Laurens unperceived and before the garrison was apprised that an Indian knew of its erection. In the course of the night, they succeed-ed in catching the horses outside of the fort; and taking off their bells, carried them into the woods, some dis-tance off. They then concealed themselves in the prairie grass, along a path leading from the fort, and in the morning commenced rattling the bells, at the farther extremity of the line of ambushment, so to induce the belief that the horses was there to be found. The stratagem succeeded. Sixteen men were sent out to bring in the horses. Allured by the sound of the bells, they kept the path, along which the Indians lay con-cealed, until they found themselves unexpectedly in the presence of an enemy, who opened upon them a de-structive fire from front and rear. Fourteen were killed on the spot, and the remaining two were taken prison-ers.

From Captain Jolly:

In page 191 (of Withers), it is stated that a party was sent out to bring in horses, etc. All the truth in that statement is that they went out, and not one of them returned. It was said this party consisted of seventeen. I was acquainted with some or all of the men who were killed. But it is a fact that there was not a horse left at Fort Laurens when the army left it. What would horses be left there for, unless it was to enrich or be taken away by the Indians? Away with such silly bombast! The fact is, they went out for the purpose of carrying in firewood, which the Army had cut before they left the place. Some forty or fifty rods from the fort, and near the bank of the river, there was a mound, behind which lay a quantity of wood, and a party had gone out several very cold mornings, and brought in wood, supposing the Indians would not be watching the fort in such very cold weather. But on the fatal morning, the Indians had concealed themselves behind the mound. And as the soldiers passed around one side of the mound, a part of the Indians came round on the other, and enclosed the wood party, so that not one escaped. I do again assert that not one horse was left there, when the army left it.

Withers, on page 192:

During the time the Indians remained about the fort, there was much sickness in the garrison; and when they were believed to have retired, the commandant detached Col. Clarke, of the Pennsylvania line, with a party of fifteen men, to escort the invalids to Fort McIntosh. They proceeded but a small distance from the gate, where they were attacked by some Indians, who had been left concealed near the fort, for the purpose of effecting further mischief. A skirmish ensued; but overpowered by numbers and much galled by the first fire, Col. Clarke could not maintain the conflict. With much difficulty, he and three others reached the fort in safety: the rest of the party were all killed.

Col. Gibson immediately marched out at the head of the greater part of the garrison, but the Indians had retreated as soon as they succeeded in cutting off the detachment under Col. Clarke, and prudence forbade to proceed in pursuit of them, as the main army was believed to be yet in the neighborhood. The dead were however brought in, and buried with the honours of war, in front of the fort gate.

In a few days after this, Gen. McIntosh arrived with a considerable body of troops and a supply of provisions for the garrison. While the savages were continuing the siege, a friendly Indian had been despatched by Col. Gibson, to acquaint Gen. McIntosh with the situation at Fort Laurens, and that without the speedy arrival of a reinforcement of men and an accession to their stock of provisions, the garrison would have to surrender; or seek a doubtful safety, by evacuating the fort and endeavoring to gain the Ohio river, in the presence of an overwhelming body of the enemy. With great promptitude, the settlers flocked to the standard of Gen. McIntosh, and loading pack horses, with abundance of provisions for the supply of the garrison at Fort Laurens, commenced a rapid march to their relief. Before their arrival, they had been relieved from the most pressing danger, by the withdrawal of the Indian army, and were only suffering from the want of flour and meat.

From Captain Jolly:

But on the 192nd page are very erroneous statements. True it is, Captain Clark was left at the fort when the Army left it for the purpose of marching in invalids and artificers, who had tarried behind the army. He endeavoured to take the advantage of very cold weather, and had marched two, three, or four miles (for I have three or four times travelled over the ground, and soon after), when he was fired on by a small party of Indians, very close, I think twenty or thirty paces. They wounded two of his men slightly. Knowing as he did, that his men were not capable of fighting Indians in their own way, [he] ordered them to reserve their fire and charge bayonet, which put the Indians to flight. And after pursuing a short distance, he called his men off, and returned to the fort, and marched all the men in that he had marched out.

A few days after General McIntosh commenced building a fort on the west bank of the Tuscarawas, three companies were detached for the purpose of escorting provision from Fort McIntosh for the purpose of supporting the troops that night, but left in the new garrison two companies of Regulars and one of Militia. The three companies returned to Fort McIntosh, and after waiting there some days for provisions, the pack horses were again loaded, and set out under the same escort for Tuscarawas, on the head of Yellow Creek.

The escort began to meet parties of the Militia, rushing on toward the Ohio with all possible speed. The company of Militia composing fully one third of the escort joined their companions and returned, leaving the two companies of Regulars (of which I was one) to guard the provisions to the Fort. Some distance down Sandy Creek, we met General McIntosh, Colonel Brodhead, and Colonel Crawford, with the Regular troops, and a few Militia, marching in tolerably good order. We encamped that night about five miles from the Fort, and the next day delivered the provision, and one company remained at the Fort, and the packhorses were escorted back to Fort McIntosh by a single company, I presume about fifty men, under the command of Lieutenant G. P. (a poor thing).

We arrived (I think) all safe at Fort McIntosh. I was with General McIntosh when he went out with the relief for Colonel Gibson. I was an eye witness to the destruction of the provisions, when General McIntosh arrived in view of the Fort. It was late in the evening when it happened. A great part of the flour was lost. A considerable part of next day was spent hunting horses, and the day following troops marched for Fort McIntosh, Major Vernon left to command the Fort. About the 1st of June he was relieved by Lieutenant-Colonel

Campbell of the Virginia line. On the 1st or 2nd of August, the garrison was evacuated. I was one of the last that left it. We arrived at Fort Pitt on the 7th.

Withers, on page 217:

> The Indian army, destined to operate against North Western Virginia, was to enter the country in two divisions of one hundred and fifty warriors each; the one crossing the Ohio near below Wheeling, the other at the mouth of Raccoon creek, about sixty miles farther up. Both were, avoiding the stronger forts, to proceed directly to Washington, then known as Catfish-town, between which place and the Ohio, the whole country was to be laid waste.

> The division crossing below Wheeling was soon discovered by scouts, who giving the alarm, caused most of the inhabitants of the more proximate settlements, to fly immediately to that place, supposing that an attack was meditated on it. The Indians, however, proceeded on the way to Washington, making prisoners of many, who though apprized that an enemy was in the country, yet feeling secure in their distance from what was expected to be the theatre of operations, neglected to use the precaution necessary to guard them against becoming prisoners to the savages.

From Captain Jolly:

Page 217, Catfish Camp. The men tied to trees, tomahawked, and scalped, were William Hawkins, Jacob Link, and Burnett. They had two young men prisoners at the same time, Jacob Miller and Presley Peak, and some females. Miller escaped from them that night. I saw him the next day. Presley Peak was taken to Detroit, and after some time came home. When the Indians tied the above victims to saplings, they said "Now we be Militia," alluding to some Indians killed by the Militia.

Withers, on page 233:

> *Near the latter part of the same month [February*
> *1782], some Indians invaded the country above Wheel-*
> *ing, and succeeded in killing a Mr. Wallace and his*
> *family, and in taking John Carpenter a prisoner. The*
> *early period of the year in which these enormities were*
> *perpetrated, the inclemency of the winter of 1781-82,*
> *and the distance of towns of hostile Indians from the*
> *theatre of these outrages, caused many to exclaim,*
> *"The Moravians have certainly done this deed." The*
> *destruction of their villages was immediately resolved,*
> *and preparations were made to carry this determina-*
> *tion into effect.*

From Captain Jolly:

John Carpenter, mentioned on page 233, a man with
whom I was intimately acquainted. He escaped from them
some distance beyond the Moravian towns, and came home. I
have heard him relate the particulars of his campaign (as he
called it), and it was truly laughable. I think he was about a
dead match for Colonel Sproat, only I presume not quite so
well educated. I have heard him repeat it so often without
variation, that I believe I could almost repeat it *verbatim*.

Withers, on page 237:

> *Two youths alone made their escape [from the*
> *massacre of the Moravians]. One of them had been*
> *knocked down and scalped, but was not killed. He had*
> *the presence of mind to lie still among the dead, until*
> *nightfall, when he crept silently forth and escaped. The*
> *other, in the confusion of the shocking scene, slipped*
> *through a trap door into the cellar, and passing out at a*
> *small window, got off unnoticed and uninjured.*

From Captain Jolly:

On page 237, we are told that two youths made their escape. One of them had been knocked down and scalped. This reminds me of what has been told to me by a man who was taken by the Indians when a lad in Wheeling. It happened soon after the murder of the Moravians. When they came to the first Indian settlements, they took him to a cabin, where he was left with an old man, an old woman, and a small boy. The old woman and the boy wept bitterly. The boy was sent out and returned with two bunches of small switches. The old man at the same time lay down on a bed with his face to the wall, and the old woman and the boy fell to work with the switches on the poor prisoner, until the old man spoke to them, and they ceased, dried up their tears, etc. The old man then showed him the cause by taking a bandage off and showing him that the boy had been tomahawked and scalped at the massacre of the Moravians. The old man told him to keep good heart. His great punishment would be running the gauntlet at the meeting, and the Indians would soon take him to Detroit, and that he would in a short time return with his friends, all of which happened in about a year. After giving him a refreshment, they took him away.

Withers, on page 246, records the following:

Here too [at the Indian town], Slover saw the dead bodies of Colonel McClalland, Major Harrison, and John Crawford; and learned that they had all been put to death but a little while before his arrival there.

From Captain Jolly:

Colonel McClellan and Major Harrison were both killed, and other relations of Colonel Crawford, but his son John was not. I was acquainted with him, and have seen him many years after Crawford's Campaign (see Withers, page 246).

Withers, on page 249:

> *Having by practice, acquired the art of loading his*
> *gun as he ran, Wetzel was indifferent how near the*
> *savages approached him, if he were out of reach of the*
> *rifles of the others. Accordingly, keeping some distance*
> *ahead of his pursuers whilst reloading his gun, he*
> *relaxed his speed until the foremost Indian had got*
> *within ten or twelve steps of him. He then wheeled,*
> *shot him dead, and again took to flight.*

From Captain Jolly:

I believe that Lewis Wetzel was the most active Rifleman
that I was ever acquainted with, and was very willing to tell
all his feats, but never pretended that he had killed more
than two Indians at the time (see Withers, page 249).

Withers, on page 262:

> *In the first of September [1782], John Lynn (a cele-*
> *brated spy and the same who had been with Captain*
> *Foreman at the time of the fatal ambuscade at Grave*
> *creek) being engaged in watching the warriors' paths,*
> *northwest of the Ohio, discovered the Indians marching*
> *with great expedition for Wheeling, and hastening to*
> *warn the inhabitants of the danger which was threat-*
> *ening them, swam the river, and reached the village,*
> *but a little while before the savage army made its*
> *appearance.*

From Captain Jolly:

I am sorry to see an error on page 262. The John Linn
mentioned there was Captain William Linn. He commanded
in 1774 under Dunmore. He and Johnson Campbell was the
means of saving a part of Foreman's Company at Graves
Creek Narrows. He served, a very conspicuous officer, a
number of campaigns from Kentucky, under Clark, Scott,

and Logan. It was said by many that he was one of the mainsprings of their campaigns. He died at last, as the fool doth. Riding alone, he was killed by Indians on Bear Grass, not far from the Falls of Ohio. So died Old Bill Linn, a brave soldier, an honest man and true friend to his country. He was an early settler on the Monongahela River, and I do not believe that Captain Bill Linn was in that part of the country at the time of the last attack on Wheeling. He certainly was in Kentucky in the year 1782, but have no doubt of his being there [Wheeling] when it was attacked in the year 1777.

Withers, on page 265:

> *Francis Duke, (son-in-law to Colonel Shepherd) was unwilling to turn his back on a people, straitened as he knew the besieged must be, and declared his intention of endeavoring to reach the fort, that he might contribute to its defence. It was useless to dissuade him from the attempt: -- he knew its danger, but he also knew their weakness, and putting spurs to his horse, rode briskly forward, calling aloud, "Open the gate, open the gate." He was seen from the fort, and the gate was loosed for his admission; but he did not live to reach it. Pierced by the bullets of the savages, he fell, to the regret of all. Such noble daring deserved a better fate.*

From Captain Jolly:

On page 265, it is asserted that Lieutenant Duke was killed in the second or last attack on Wheeling, but the fact is that on the 1st of September in the year 1777, Frank Duke and his brother-in-law William Shepherd was killed. The particulars as respects the warriors' attacks on Wheeling, I refer to Captain John Mills on Wheeling, a veteran of the Revolution, and Thomas Miller of Monroe County, Ohio. The latter received sixteen or seventeen wounds at one volley. Some years ago the particulars of that was published in *The American Friend*, as I received it from the mouth of the said Thomas Miller.

I believe that Captain William Linn gave the alarm when the Indians were approaching the Fort in 1777, and George Green gave the alarm in 1782. And I do assert that Lieutenant Duke's widow was married to Levi Springer of Fayette County, Pennsylvania, before the Indians made the last attack on Wheeling Fort.

It is a pity that so many murders that have been committed should be passed without notice: the Simms family at Fish Creek, Anderson's family, Belleville, a family by the name of Jolly on Wheeling, the killing of John Walker and wounding Lieutenant Biggs at the mouth of Indian Wheeling (Lt. Biggs lives now on Pipe Creek, Belmont County), the killing of Captain John Wetzel and another on or near Fish Creek and the remarkable adventure of Lewis Wetzel on that occasion -- that has been within my own knowledge --, the killing of [Mills] and taking John Wetzel prisoner, and the killing of three Indians by Hamilton Karr and Isaac Williams, at the mouth of Graves Creek, and retaking the prisoner.

In the Spring of the year 1783, two Indians came to Graves Creek flats, and after taking some flour from an old lady, went up Wheeling and killed Redford and Death. There is nothing said about the wounding and miraculous escape of Nathan Parr, late of this county. A slave belonging to Philip Witten, late of this county, was taken prisoner by two Indians. He killed one and made his escape.

In the last of August or the first of September in 1777, the Indians killed some children near Shepherd's Fort, took a lad prisoner. He was about eleven years old, and lived with the Indians eleven years. He went in company with two Indians into Kentucky, and was accessory to the death of both the Indians. He lives in Belmont County, Ohio. Some part of the above account was published some years ago in *The American Friend*, which I believe is the most correct account that can possibly be obtained at this time. If I should ever feel myself able to write, I will add a little to the narrative of Lewis Wetzel, which is particularly within my own knowledge.

Withers, on page 306:

Among the few interesting incidents which occurred in the upper country, during this year, was the captivity and remarkable escape of two brothers, John and Henry Johnson -- the former thirteen, the latter eleven years of age. They lived at a station on the west side of the Ohio river near above Indian Short creek; and being at some distance from the house, engaged in the sportive amusements of youth, became fatigued and seated themselves on an old log for the purposes of resting. They presently observed two men coming towards them, whom they believed to be white men from the station until they approached so close as to leave no prospect of escape by flight, when to their great grief they saw that two Indians were beside them. They were made prisoners, and taken about four miles, when after partaking of some roasted meat and parched corn given them by their captors, they were arranged for the night, by being placed between the two Indians and each encircled in the arms of the one next him.

From Captain Jolly:

The account of the two boys taken prisoners, I expect, is correct. Henry Johnson, I believe, is a respectable character, lives now in Woodfield (see page 306).

The Narrative
of Lydia Boggs Shepherd
Cruger (1766-1867)
Covering the Years
1772-1786

I N JUNE 1772, [there was] a very great freshet in the Ohio, and Jonathan Zane marked a tree to where the water backed up to the Falls of Wheeling, near the Forks. I think the Zanes and Wetzel and Bonnett emigrations did not settle with their families until the spring of 1773.

Captain John Boggs, born on Connodoquin, a tributary of the Susquehanna, in 1736, on the 31st of March, died in February 1824 in his eighty-eighth year. He removed to Berkeley when he was a child, in Back Creek, a tributary of Potomac. In 1768 with his family settled in the neighborhood of Colonel William Crawford on Youghioghany, and in 1771 near Beeson's Fort (now Uniontown), etc. He was on the Tuscarawas campaign.

In 1776, Captain John Boggs with others went down the Ohio River to Kentucky -- met Cornstalk and others on the bank of the river. All preferred peace, but were jealous of each other. Boggs made improvements in Kentucky, but the Revolution coming on, he neglected them.

JOHN BOGGS AND THE FIRST SIEGE OF WHEELING

It was on Monday, the 1st of September. That was muster day at Catfish Camp, under Captain John Boggs and Captain Reazon Virgin, and while mustering, towards evening, an express came that Wheeling was attacked, and Boggs and

Virgin and their men immediately resolved to start off, and marched all night, and reached Wheeling early Tuesday morning. All the Indians had gone. They helped to bury the dead and haul off the swollen dead cattle into the river.

THE FIRST SIEGE OF WHEELING

It was the 1st of September 1777. In the morning early, Dr. David W. Mahony designed to remove away, and sent out one Boyd with two negroes up the hill, to find the horses to remove on. Boyd was shot and scalped by Indians in ambush, and the negroes escaped to the fort. This was the first intelligence of the approach of the Indians. Then Captains Ogle and Mason, each having a company of militia there -- Mason from the waters of Tenmile, near Washington, Pennsylvania --, [went out] with a party, about three fourths of a mile, where the Indians [were] in ambush in pawpaw bushes on the creek bottom, and while the men were hunting for the trail, the Indians arose from their covert around them, and fired upon the whites -- shot them down.

Mason received a flesh wound in the hip, and hid himself in a fallen treetop, full of green leaves. The Indians hunted all around him, he seeing them. In the night he escaped to some neighboring fort. Captain Ogle escaped to the cornfield with a wounded man, and [they] concealed themselves in the high horse weeds, and while there, a wounded Indian, blood running down, and crying, and another Indian with him, both sitting on the fence within a handsel of Ogle, and Ogle expecting every moment to be discovered, he lay with his gun cocked, intending if discovered to sell his life as dearly as possible.

Those Indians remained on the fence, and finally went away. In the night, Ogle took the wounded man with him into the fort. Three of the men, William Shepherd (oldest son of Colonel David Shepherd), Hugh McConnell, and Thomas Glenn, started from the defeated spot for the fort, and young Shepherd (only nineteen) as he neared the fort, his foot caught in a grape vine and threw him, and before he could recover, the Indians tomahawked and scalped him. Glenn was chased above the fort a little distance up river, and was overtaken and killed. McConnell reached the fort. John Caldwell escaped to Shepherd's Fort, six miles from Wheeling at the Forks of Wheeling, where the neighborhood forted, though Colonel Shepherd was himself at Wheeling. [The] others escaped.

Town lots had been sold, and several had built cabins and lived in them outside Fort Henry; and at this alarm -- unexpected -- the people flew to the Fort, leaving all their property in their cabins -- all [of] which was plundered, and some of the cabins burned, and others were seized and occupied by the Indians, from which to fight.

Francis Duke (a son-in-law of Colonel Shepherd and Deputy Commissary) came from the Beech Bottom Station, above, about noon, and came among the Indians before he was aware of danger, and made a dash for the Fort, and was shot dead some 75 yards from the Fort -- so near that the Indians did not venture for his scalp until after nightfall, when they dragged his body into one of the cabins, and scalped and stripped him.

The Indians shot down large numbers of cattle, hogs, geese; and took a great many horses. Soon after dark, they decamped. [There were] thought to have been two hundred Indians. Probably [Simon] Girty was not with them.

Major Samuel McCulloch came from Vanmeter's Fort on Short Creek, and hemmed in unexpectedly by Indians, went down the bank, his horse sliding on his shanks, and near the bottom jumping and striking on his feet. McCulloch escaped back to Vanmeter's. I have no knowledge of his having any men with him. If Colonel Andrew Swearingen ever went to Wheeling with a small reinforcement [however], it was in 1777.

FOREMAN'S DEFEAT

Foreman and his company were from the South Branch of Potomac. [They] went to see if there were any Indian signs. The fort at Grove Creek had been deserted before the attack on Wheeling, and [they] had gone there for safety. When Foreman's party left Wheeling, Moses Shepherd, only fourteen years old, went along half a mile to beat the drum for Foreman's men. [He] was so affected at the defeat, that he would never play on the drum afterwards.

I think the defeat was September 22nd, as William Cruger thinks. The Indians doubtless saw them on their way down. They camped all night at Grove Creek. Next morning, they started on [their] return, playing along, some knocking off hats, and careless. They were attacked. William Cullens had his right leg broken above the ankle, and scrambled nearly up the hill. Linn helped him up (Linn heard the firing and holloaing and came running -- Jacob Wetzel was too young to take part then), and left him at a spring at the top of the hill, and gave him some biscuit he had in his pouch, and promised to return for him. Linn went to Shepherd's Fort, got a horse, and alone went for Cullens (perhaps the second night), and there mounted him on the horse and took him through the woods, his leg dangling as they jumped logs, etc. A little before day, they reached Shepherd's. Linn was a most excellent woodsman. William Cruger heard Colonel Shepherd mention this, and I heard Cullens say the same.

Two or three days after Foreman's defeat, while Shepherd's and others were breaking up, William Grist, living on Peter's Run of Little Wheeling, broke up. He had been forting at Shepherd's, and when breaking up, Grist and his family took the lead in going towards Catfish Camp, wishing to stop at their cabin and get some things left there. They were fallen upon. Rachel Grist, some eleven years old, was knocked down with a war club and scalped. James, a lad of seven or eight, was killed, and John Grist Jr. was taken prisoner. Rachel was found, conveyed to Catfish, and the doctor trepanning, she recovered, and afterwards married Captain Henry Jolly, who had served three years in the War to the eastward (James Jolly, his brother with him, died of camp fever), and they raised three children. She eventually died from the effects of that wound. Peter Jolly, Henry's father, settled near Catfish about 1773.

IN 1780

In the fall of 1780, three men went from Buffalo Creek over the Ohio on a scout -- Jacob Fankler, one Perrin, and Lucas Schermerhorn. Fankler was a cowardly young man, very tall, and when all three lay down before the fire at night, he desired to sleep in the middle, and being tall crooked up his legs to have the blanket cover. Some Indians shot at them, and two balls passed through both of Fankler's thighs as they struck above the others. Perrin was also badly wounded. Schermerhorn jumped up unharmed, without his gun, and ran off a little distance in the dark and trees. The Indians seemed to be afraid at first to approach the camp. Young Fankler cried bitterly, while Perrin holloaed out to the Indians to come and tomahawk them and put them out of their miseries. This was done. Schermerhorn escaped, but to fall a sacrifice to the enemy some two years after, together with John Kinser, on Buffalo Creek.

Captain McIntyre, who had the fight of 1780 [of which Mrs. William Cruger has no particular recollections -- LCD] subsequent to the Revolutionary War, was while in the oriental country, taken by the Turks, being a very handsome man, was fancied by all of the noble ladies, who castrated him and made a room servant of him, and he never returned to his native land. Many were the mortified feelings.

THE SUMMER OF 1781

On the 30th of July 1781, Captain John Boggs then living on Buffalo Creek, twelve Indians came and hid themselves among the stacks of grain in the field. William Boggs, then in his eighteenth year (who with Wetzel at Wheeling toma-hawked Killbuck, the chief), went to the field to drive out the calves, and was taken by five Indians, while the other seven (it was a foggy morning) came towards the house, and Captain Boggs seized his gun and kept the Indians at bay, several times shot at by the Indians, until the family ran half a mile to James Newell's, and then Captain Boggs escaped.

Then all the families in that location again commenced forting at William Sparks's (father of Robert Sparks, for Robert was in Captain Ogle's company on Brodhead's Campaign in the spring of 1781, and Ogle lived on Short Creek). In this flight, the present Mrs. Cruger had previously been snake-bitten and with difficulty could wobble around, but she ran to Newell's and was the first to reach there, not once thinking of her disabled limb.

In August 1781, Captain Boggs removed to Wheeling, and was there when the Indian party appeared there, as already stated, in September. A few weeks after, the same party, under Sam Gray, a halfbreed who had taken young Boggs, appeared and killed Captain Sam Teter and another man in the heart of Buffalo.

The party that took Boggs, previous to reaching Captain Boggs's, on the Dutch Fork of Buffalo, met Daniel Harrison and a negro, both on horseback, fired at them, Harrison wounded in the hip. Both escaped. Harrison lay in a clump of willows all night. They chased the negro, etc.

In the summer of 1781, Andrew Zane and one Lewis were passing the same rocks [where Stalnaker was killed the next year], above Wheeling Narrows, and from behind which Indians fired and killed Lewis, and slightly wounded Zane. He effected his escape.

William Boggs, when taken in 1781, was tied to stakes at night, where it rained on him. When reaching the Indians, he ran the gauntlet, two times a day. He took the ague. He was greatly afraid he would be recognized as aiding in killing Killbuck. He was finally, with young Presley Peak and others, sold to the British at Detroit, and exchanged, and got home after eighteen months' captivity.

In 1781, when Link's blockhouse was taken, and young Peak and Miss Hawkins were captured, Miss Hawkins when in captivity married a Frenchman, raised some children, and when her husband died, she returned to her friends awhile, but not liking it, she again went to where she had lived a semi-barbarous life, and lived and died there.

SEPTEMBER 1781 ATTACK ON WHEELING

One hundred Indians appeared in the afternoon. Two lads of about ten and twelve, William Ryan and David Glenn, were playing at the spring, at the foot of the hill at the river, then swampy. The Indians chased the boys, and while crossing a log, Ryan was knocked off into the mud with a tomahawk, and they killed him. They overtook Glenn and captured him, and asked him if the people had any cannon, and the boy said they had a wooden cannon, and so they had -- banded with four bands. That afternoon, towards night, it was for the first time loaded and fired. It burst without firing the ball. They found it on the river bank after the Indians had gone.

After young Ryan was killed, and Glenn taken, they ran up and wounded George Reagan through the wrist. He was a rod or so from the first gate. They then ran off instantly.

This same party then went to the blockhouse of Jacob Link, on the Middle Fork of Wheeling, fourteen miles above Wheeling Fort. They attacked Link's and took it, and killed him, one Miller, and perhaps others. Link's wife and child were with Moses Shepherd and one of the Wetzels, and a snake-bit man passing from Wetzel's to the settlements around Catfish, and [they] had left Link's in the afternoon, where they had stopped and shot at a mark. They went on, and that evening the Indians came and took the place.

The next day, the Indians went to the Peaks' high up the Dutch Fork of Buffalo, and succeeded in capturing Presley Peak, about seventeen, and William Hawkins, and one Blackburn, and probably killed some. Hawkins had a family within hearing, and Hawkins begged they would not kill him, that he would go with them, and get his wife and children, and go live with them; and they then started for Hawkins's.

But those others had heard the firing at Peaks' and becoming alarmed, had fled. The snake-bit man had been left there, and he and Elizabeth Hawkins, a young lady then sick, ran off, and being unable to go far, the man's wound being too severe, hid in the cornfield. They were however tracked, the man killed, and Miss Hawkins taken. Mrs. Hawkins and her other three children (one an infant of two weeks at her breast) flew into the thick hazel bushes, and could not be tracked, and escaped.

Then the Indians took about half a mile from Hawkins's, on the ridge, tied Hawkins and Blackburn each to a dogwood sapling, tomahawked and scalped them, and left them there fastened with their bodies erect. The Indians assigned as a reason for killing them, that Hawkins had red hair and the other black! About young Peak -- he was kept seventeen months.

IN MARCH 1782

In March 1782, Captain Boggs, living third below Wheeling at Boggs Run, saw signs of two Indians near his house and sugar camp. Boggs had two soldiers from Wheeling stationed with him, Hugh Cameron and another. Boggs immediately moved with his family to Wheeling. The soldiers remained of their own accord in the camp to make molasses. The two Indians crept upon them and shot them. Cameron was wounded in the hand, and from fear did not try to escape, and was taken. The other escaped. Subsequently, Cameron's remains were found near the sugar camp.

David Morgan, ploughing, with some of his children with him, discovered two Indians posted at the fence, and managed to send his children to the house, then killed one Indian, and mortally wounded the other. The Indians first shot at him, missed -- all tried, one of the Indians loading behind a small tree with a crook in it. Morgan shot him. The other and Morgan scuffled, the Indian on top (who first threw his tomahawk at Morgan). The Indian tried to get out his knife, which Morgan managed to seize, and nearly cut the Indian's hand off, and plunged the knife into the Indian's body, twisting it around.

The Indian went off. Morgan went to his house, and returned with others. The Indian had crept into a tree top. Morgan shot him. He found the Indian had pulled the knife from the wound, and drove it into the earth full-length. Morgan skinned and tanned their hides, made pants and vest, and razor strops, boasting it was the best he ever had, was very best, etc., and every good soldier should have such a razor strop.

THE SUMMER OF 1782

In the forenoon of the 30th of July 1782, while Hamilton Karr, Henry Smith, and Thomas Mills (no connection of him of the same name who was killed the spring before) went to the Ohio side of the river, to Glenn's Run, four miles above Wheeling, gigging fish, and caught a catfish which weighed 87 1/2 pounds, and while taking the fish from the bearded prongs, and near shore, they were fired on by a party of about thirty Indians, and Mills was shot all to pieces, in his body and both arms and both legs, all flesh wounds, except a bad wound in his left leg at and above the knee, which shattered the bones -- seventeen wounds and two slight skips. After two years' disability, he recovered and got well, leaving a stiff knee.

Mills fell, Smith slightly wounded in the groin, and Smith jumped out into the water. The Indians threw down their empty guns, and with their tomahawks ran into the water, but Karr kept them off with his spear (or gig), and at the same time pushed off the canoe, and the Indians ran back for the guns. Smith now got into the canoe, and the Indians soon got their guns loaded and commenced firing on the boat, and Smith would jump out, but Karr kept pushing off, and finally got beyond reach.

Andrew Zane and James Fulton in a canoe were going up a-fishing, but were not yet so high up, and put off and were fired at distantly. When the Mills boat reached Wheeling, it was half filled with water, bullet holes in the canoe, sand and blood -- and their fish!

As Zane and Fulton came near the island, they spied out the Indians, and the people on the island fled to the Fort. Mills was not only shot down but was half drowned in the water. Karr was unhurt. Mills in his old age drew a pension. He lived till he was eighty years old.

The same party of Indians crossed the Ohio the same day, and about [that time], Major Sam and John McCulloch were going to the mouth of Short Creek from Vanmeter's Fort, Sam ahead. They were fired at, and Sam was shot through the kidneys and dropped dead. John dashed on, and looking back, seeing an Indian in the act of scalping his brother, John fired and killed him, and escaped.

That evening, a party went from Vanmeter's and got Major McCulloch's body -- his heart was taken out -- and buried [it] at Vanmeter's. He was raised on the South Branch of Potomac. The wife of Ebenezer Zane was his sister (Elizabeth McCulloch). McCulloch came out with his father, John McCulloch, and settled on Short Creek in 1774; the father died not long after. There were in the family Elizabeth, Samuel, John, Abraham, George, and Sarah (married Lieutenant Jacob Coleman and went first to Kentucky, then Indiana).

Major Samuel McCulloch was in the Assembly in the winter of 1780-1781. He made his jump in 1777, went out scouting and in much service, was on Brodhead's Campaign in 1781. He had been married to Miss May Mitchell but six months (sister of Alexander Mitchell), left no children. He was about thirty years old, middle size, straight, fair complexion.

Early in August 1782, William Neisinger and Jacob Leffler took a canoe and went down the river spying. At night they reached the mouth of Settle Grave Creek (painted and dressed like Indians), and there in the willows they fastened their canoe and lay down in it and went asleep. In the night, Indians crept up, killed Neisinger with their tomahawks, and Leffler jumped up, and seizing a paddle, and as he said "knocked the Indians to the south and west" -- and finally received a tomahawk wound, cutting off two small fingers on one hand, as it gripped the paddle.

He jumped out, and not able to swim, kept along near shore, near the willows, part of the way chin deep, and it being dark, escaped. He heard the Indians moving along the shore, and the next morning was foggy, which greatly favored his escape. He waded about a mile, before he ventured on the bank. Next forenoon he reached Wheeling, and his hand became so bad, he went to Pittsburgh for medical aid.

THE SIEGE OF WHEELING, 1782

The people in the Fort became careless, and even neglected to close the fort gates of night. Jonathan Zane said he would not stand sentry: he was not afraid. And others said they would not watch for Jonathan Zane's family if he wouldn't do it for himself: they were as brave as he, etc.

The siege commenced about sun an hour high, Monday, September 11th -- at all events, the 11th. Ten days before this, as was afterwards learned, the spies of the Indians were spying of nights around the Fort, and two or three nights before the attack, two Indians were seen in the Fort by two or three of the women, who gave intelligence. But the men of the Fort scouted at the idea. (The women had got up in the night to go out and make water, and came near urinating on them! -- old Mrs. Connard was one). The men said the women were half blind and couldn't tell in the night an Indian from a hog and calf, etc.

On the morning of the 11th, a damp morning, Stephen Burkam and one Wright started from the Fort to Washington, and got three or four miles, when they saw trails in the woods which they thought were made by Indians, and thought they heard the picking of flints, and returned to Wheeling and reported. Just about the same time, Andrew Zane and some men returned from about the same place where Burkam and Wright had seen signs. They had gone for a keg of whiskey which Zane had left a few days before when alarmed. They got the keg, and said the trails were made by cattle, etc.

On Wheeling Island (three miles long and nearly one wide) were several cabins which the people had wintered in, and where they had cornfields, and were cleaning out these cabins in which to move, before doing which, however, it was deemed best to send out a couple of Spies on Brodhead's Trail to see if there were any signs. Hamilton Karr and Peter Neisinger went early that morning, and went several miles out beyond what is now St. Clairsville, and seeing no sign, killed a cub bear -- wasted the paws for a meal -- and killed a spike (one-year) buck, and on return, Neisinger, with his buck slung on his back, discovered near the present St. Clairsville where the Indians had marched in three lines, and, alarmed, they hastened to Wheeling, and Neisinger did not [avail] himself of his deer.

About 3 o'clock in the afternoon, the two Spies (having gone down Indian Wheeling) crossed to the Island, and fired their guns by way of alarm, and soon repeated it. The Spies reported that the Indians were coming, from three to five hundred. It was suggested that Captain John Boggs should go to Catfish Camp to alarm the country, and to get aid, and it was known that Colonel James Marshel (who lived and died at Charleston, at the mouth of Buffalo, and had a mill there) was collecting men for a campaign against the Sandusky Towns.

When about a mile up the river, he met Abraham McCulloch and gave the intelligence. McCulloch came on a short distance, when he heard the alarm gun fired, then turned and overtook Captain Boggs, and that night went to Short Creek, and early next morning to Catfish Camp.

Instant preparations were made for defense. Lieutenant Matthew Neely, while stationed at Pittsburgh, in bathing, discovered in the river a swivel gun, carrying a pound ball, and had it got out. It was spiked and doubtless thrown into the river by the French in 1758. Neely claimed it as private property, and in the fall of 1781, was after a while ordered with some twenty-five men to Wheeling, and remained three or four months, and brought the swivel with him. He was ordered there in consequence of the Indians' appearing at Wheeling in September 1781, and when he returned to Pittsburgh left the swivel, thinking it needed.

About the center of the Fort, a platform or battery was erected, a four-square log pen to overshoot the pickets, [built] with portholes, and the pen built above for the safety of the women. The men, women, and children all went with buckets to the river, not liking to venture to the spring next to the hill by the woods -- [Mrs. Cruger] aided in carrying water -- and then all the vessels were filled, and just as they were concluding this, a party of some sixty Indians, sun an hour high, made their appearance on the Island and gave distant shouts at those carrying water.

Balls were run, camp hatchets stuck in the pickets, along the portholes, with orders for the women, if the Indians undertook to scale the pickets, to chop their fingers off. The Indians soon surrounded the Fort, three hundred Indians, a company of the Queen's Rangers, fifty men, under Captain Pratt and Ensign McGillen, from Detroit. About a hundred yards above the spring, behind a large sugar tree, one of the enemy posted himself, presenting the British colors. (Just before the Indians surrounded the Fort, Cobe Sullivan and two others of Clark's men luckily reached there in a canoe on their way down to the Falls of Ohio, and lent a helping hand.)

The Indians had crossed (except the sixty who went to the Island, and expected to have found the people at work there in their cabins, but in this was disappointed) at the shoal at the upper end of Boggs Island, three miles below Wheeling, and passed up and crossed Wheeling Creek half a mile from the mouth at the head of the backwaters.

When the flag was seen, the swivel was fired at the flag. This emblem now disappeared. At this instant all the people in the Fort raised a defiant yell -- men, women, and children, all ordered to do so, throwing up hats, caps, brooms, sticks, and everything within their reach. Then even the smallest children, too small to comprehend it, joined most lustily in this bravado, some hollering "Come on! We are ready for you!" and shooting occasionally. All this was done to convey the idea that the Fort was well defended by brave and fearless men. Nor were the enemy silent. They too mingled their yells and whoops with those within the Fort, and shooting down the cattle, hogs, etc. And for a time all was noise and confusion. (Just before the cannon was fired on the flag, an old red cow came passing by in the road. The flagbearer gave her a blow with the flagstaff, and she ran down to the Fort, and was let in.)

The strength of the garrison: Andrew and Jonathan Zane, Peter Neisinger, Hamilton Karr, Matthew Karr (the father), and Alex McDowell, James Smith Sr., Henry and Thomas Smith (sons), Conrad Stoub, Jacob Reagen, James Clark, George Reagen, Thomas Mills Sr. and son Edward, Henry and Frank Clark, John Tate, Conrad Wheat, James Salten, Stephen Burkam and Edward Knight, Sullivan and his two men -- and four lads not exceeding thirteen years of age, viz: James Boggs, Matthew and George Karr and James Smith Jr.

At Ebenezer Zane's house, sixty yards distant from the fort, were Ebenezer and Silas Zane, George Green and Andrew Scott, and also a Guinea Negro, Sam, in Zane's kitchen. These constituted the strength of the garrison.

The enemy had learned the year before, from David Glenn, that the pickets at the Fort were quite rotten, and they only had a wooden cannon. That was then true. The cannon was busted the evening after young Glenn was captured, and in the spring of 1782, finding the pickets decayed, they threw up a dirt embankment against the pickets on both sides, but much the most inside, so that it was made to answer a double purpose, strengthening the pickets and forming an embankment on which to stand (four feet high) to shoot out of the portholes. Now when the cannon was first fired, Captain Pratt was heard to say (as related by the negro taken afterwards, and the two young men who escaped, Moore and the other, and ran off to Tenmile Creek), "That is no wooden cannon -- it is as good a metal cannon as was ever fired: it is no use to try to take them -- they are in good spirits and will fight."

It was a new moon, and it shone for two hours after dark. During this period the British and Indians crept up into a deep gully washed by rains, on the river on the western side of the Fort, and almost at the very base of the picketing. Here they could post themselves in safety, for those within could not bring their guns to shoot into this gully.

For two hours a most serio-ludicrous scene took place. Captain Pratt now called out, announcing who he was, called upon the garrison to surrender, promising as good quarters and treatment as King George could afford, and that he was disposed to be kind if they would capitulate: and he added, that they had three hundred Indians, and fifty of the Queen's Rangers from Detroit, and the next day they would have fifteen hundred more, with cannon to batter down the picketing, that they were well aware of the weakness of the garrison, for it had been very well ascertained by their spies, who only two or three nights before were within the very Fort itself, were well nigh being showered by the old women when they had occasion to get up and go out in the night -- that they knew full well that the Fort was defended chiefly by women and children. But if the garrison should obstinately refuse to surrender, they might rely upon it that, when taken by storm, as they would be, no quarters would be granted. All should be massacred, and they could blame no one but themselves. "Your blood," said they, "be on your own hands." Ensign McGillen and others spoke to the same effect.

Jonathan Zane, from the northwest bastion, in return replied, "We have no favors to ask of such cutthroat savages, villains, Tories, and fiendish devils as you -- rely upon it. We would never sink basely to surrendering to such a contemptible foe. We will never be taken alive -- and if taken at all, it will be fighting in the last ditch. In King George's name, you have graciously promised us good quarters: as for King George, we most heartily detest his very name, and couple it only with the blackest infamy, and the quarters you so generously promise us, are such as you gave Colonel Crawford and his men."

"And you, Ensign McGilles, have informed us that you are from Scotland. In God's name, have you come all that distance to join savages in their inhuman and indiscriminate warfare against helpless women and children? Are these the laurels you seek to bedeck your brow? You offer rewards to your savage allies for American scalps, of all ages and sexes: is this the conduct of a great and Christian people?"

"We have no confidence in British promises, and shall certainly not heed them, nor do we fear for your threats. We have sent for assistance, and will give you hot work enough for you shortly. Come on, you heathen wretches, and we will soon have your scalps dangling over the gates of our Fort."

Not a little blackguarding now ensued, in which Betsey Wheat, a bold, rough, fearless Dutch girl, figured prominently. Passes at wit and low jesting were briskly interchanged. One of the British called out to Betsey Wheat, who had given them many a hard joke, to run her arm down the cow's throat in the Fort bawling for her calf, and begged to know if they had any whiskey in the Fort, and if so, how they made it?

"Yes," said Betsey, "we have plenty. We distill it in a large camp kettle, dip it out with ladles, and damn you, you shall have it as hot as you like, and if you prefer it first to pass through the bullet holes, you shall have it in that form."

"What is your name?" said one of the British. "I tell you my name?" said Betsey, "Never to such contemptuous ruffians. You [bastards] go to hell! You think we can't shoot you in our present position? In time, we will stone you out of it." The Indians, who took no part in the sallies at wit, seemed heartily to enjoy the conversation.

The moon was now disappearing, and the heroine Betsey Wheat, and I, with the others, got all the stones, pulled up the hearths, and commenced a shower of rocks over the picketing into the gully, and its occupants gladly decamped, several of them with sore heads.

The British and Indians now with fife and drum marched up to attack the fort, and commenced a heavy fire, chiefly directed against the north or up-river end, as if to concentrate their fire and intimidate the garrison into a surrender. The firing was very brisk, with slight intercessions, all night.

The women, including me, were some of the time running bullets and necking them, and at other times forted at portholes, ready to use the hatchets in case the enemy should attempt to scale the pickets. Betsey Wheat, the whole night and the remainder of the siege, took her place at a porthole, performing well her part with a musket.

During the night, the swivel was fired sixteen times, and the report jarred down two of the pickets that had rotted at the lower ends, but on account of the proximity of some peach-trees on the outside, the outside embankment was omitted, and Peter Neisinger seeing it crept through the opening, and put them up, screened from discovery by the peach-trees covered with leaves and the darkness of the night, and got into the Fort at the sallyport gate near by. The Indians did, during the night, attempt to push down the picketing, expecting to have done so with ease, as young Glenn had told them, but in this they were disappointed.

The women also poured out molten lead on the ground and cut it into slugs for the muskets, for some few had no rifles, and there was no shot.

There was a blockhouse, with a blacksmith shop adjoining it, occupied by James Reagen and Conrad Stoup, Henry and Francis Clark, with their families, who were resolved to defend it. But after dark, before the attack, they abandoned the house and sought safety in the Fort. This house the Indians took possession of. It was not over forty yards from the sallyport gate and they fired from the second storey, and the swivel was leveled against it, and knocked the roof off, dislodging the Indians. John Tate, an old artillery man in the Revolutionary War, managed the swivel, and did it well.

North of the Fort was a cornfield, and above it a hemp patch, which latter was pulled and shucked. This the Indians got, and placed next to the picketing on the river side of the Fort, and fired squibs into it, but it was not sufficiently big to burn. This attempt to fire the Fort was not observed, as the night was dark, and this firing was directed against the north end, where the flashing of the guns would only light. But in the Fort were several "squirts" made of gun-barrels on purpose to force water a considerable distance to put out any attemp to burn the Fort, and these would have been used effectually.

The four boys, James Boggs, Matthew and George Karr, and James Smith, with their heavy public musket, heavily charged, and on the platform, were kicked off in the ditch made by excavating dirt for the embankment, and half filled with mud and water. Wet as drowned rats, they did not desist, but took position in the bastions, and when knocked back were secure from the water and mud. These boys acted heroically.

Cobe Sullivan, while fighting bravely, was wounded in the foot. Zane's house was also fired upon, without injury -- a large hewed log house, strong puncheon bulleproof doors and window shutters; and in the kitchen adjoining Zane's house, was Old Sam and his termagant wife. In the kitchen was a porthole and a small hole in the chimney, through which an Indian shot Sam slightly on the foot. Poor Sam grumbled sorely at this mishap.

Tuesday the 12th -- This day the Indians fired but occasional distant shots, one of which broke the leg of one of the cows, and they had to kill her. There were several cows in the Fort, and thus saved.

In the forenoon, a negro was discovered lying beside the cornfield fence near Rigger's house and shot -- a single shot, slightly wounding him in the breast. He begged for quarters, and dragged his fusee along with him, and when he came in, fearing he might be a spy, and have used this stratagem to get into the Fort, and might seek an opportunity to jump out, they pinioned him. He said he had been captured by the Indians on Holston, and declared he sought that way to get into the Fort; and that he had been ordered to set the hemp on fire the preceeding night, and had failed. He told of the designs of the enemy, etc.

The Indians at Rigger's (Reagan's) house, and in some of the cabins on the Island, found some white petticoats that had been left in the flight to the Fort preceeding the attack. These garments the Indians put on and made a female parade, keeping at a respectful distance on the Island and on the sandbar. Small arms were discharged at them and once the swivel was levelled at them.

During the day, Jacob Lefler, who had gone to Pittsburgh to get his hand cured, returned, and without knowing of the Fort's investment, and was close up, in the woods about two miles from the Fort, when they overtook and killed him. The Indians raised the scalp-halloa, and boasted of having killed one of the Spies.

Near mid-day, having exhausted the powder at Zane's house, Molly Scott ran over from Zane's to the Fort, sixty yards, for a supply. Captain Boggs had charge of the magazine, and in his absence the magazine was open, and I went in with her and poured out some tenths into Molly's tow apron, and she ran back. She was not fired at going or returning. The Indians were on the hillside and elsewhere too far to have shot with any effect. [Mrs. Cruger in this says she couldn't be mistaken, and Major Bonnett corroborates it as a fact he has long understood -- LCD]

This day the Indians killed what cattle they could find. During the day, the enemy got some howels out of some of the cabins, made a hickory cannon, and splitting the piece and hollowing it out with the howel, a small hand adze, and chaining it together. Sullivan in his canoe had left some swivel balls. These the Indians got.

After night, this new engine was put to the test. The report was a mere squash, which caused a hearty laugh by its projectors. Those in the Fort bawled out, "Is that your British cannon?" The firing was kept up all night, but the enemy were evidently disheartened, and did not make the efforts they did the first night.

On Wednesday morning, while the enemy were only seen on the Island, some of the men, half starved, went out to the hand-mill in front of Zane's house, to grind corn, and were fired at by the Indians from the Island. The men would dodge at the flash, but the distance was too great to render their shots dangerous.

The Indians were now withdrawing, and the men would call out to them, to come back and take their cannon. By 10 o'clock, the enemy had all disappeared, to the great joy and relief of all. During the investment, amid the care and excitement, little was eaten by any. Corn was now ground, and bread speedily made. The besieged lost not a man: Sullivan and "Old Sam" only were wounded. Sullivan had his wound bound up, and immediately resumed his place at the porthole. It was not known how many the enemy lost. Blood was plenty, but whether of their killed and wounded, or only of the cattle, hogs, sheep, and dogs, could not be known.

Before noon, Captain Boggs, with forty men from Catfish Camp, arrived at full gallop, Colonel David and Captain Eleaser Williamson and Moses Shepherd among them. The dead cattle were dragged into the river, and these men returned to their farms. About a hundred of the Indians went to Rice's Fort on the Dutch Fork of Buffalo.

The canoe and cannon balls (and some apples also) brought by Cobe Sullivan's party were hastily abandoned as they landed, the Indians throwing the balls into the river, which being shallow, they were subsequently recovered and carried down to the Falls of Ohio. It was one of these balls that was used by the Indians in their wooden cannon. The forty men who came did not reach Wheeling till the third day after the attack. They were troubled in getting together.

COLONEL DAVID SHEPHERD

His father, Thomas Shepherd, came while a young man from England, went to Berkeley County, Virginia, and there married Miss Elizabeth Vanmeter, daughter of William Vanmeter, a very wealthy German then settled in Berkeley. David was the oldest of ten children, born in January 1734, died 2d of February 1795, a little over 61 years of age, and is buried in the family burial ground at the Forks of Big and Little Wheeling. Shepherdstown, Virginia, took its name from Thomas Shepherd, where his plantation, a large one, was given him by his father-in-law, Vanmeter.

Colonel David Shepherd was married to Miss Rachel Teague, and in the spring of 1774 moved to the Forks of Wheeling, where he purchased the settlement right of Silas Zane. Dunmore's War breaking out, Colonel Shepherd removed to the Crossings of Youghiogany, near what is now Connellsville. In the fall of 1774 he returned to Wheeling.

Colonel Shepherd made a fort on his place, to which the up-creek people resorted, erected a mill in 1775, a single-geared mill. He commanded at the Siege of Wheeling in 1777, and commanded some men on a Tuscarawas campaign in 1778. Captain Boggs went out also on the Tuscarawas campaign. There was some little fighting. An old Dutchman killed an Indian and put the scalp into his wallet with his beads, and swimming over the Tuscarawas, the old man lost his bag or wallet, greatly to his mortification. Andrew Robertson, an Irishman, was lost: he disappeared.

Colonel Shepherd was out on Brodhead's campaign in April 1781. He was not at the Siege of Wheeling in 1782. In the fall of 1777, when Shepherd broke up his fort, he removed his family to the neighborhood of Catfish Camp, where he remained five years. He spent much of his time in Wheeling, tending his mill. His old houses were burnt, but the mill was unmolested, except that sometimes the Indians would set it running and leave it.

He was in the Virginia Legislature in the Session of 1785, and perhaps two or three previous Sessions, a Justice, a Sheriff, etc. -- the first. An Episcopalian. A little short of six feet, corpulent, 240 pounds weight, light complexion, blue eyes -- great good sense, brave, honest, liberal and benevolent, cheerful and good natured, greatly beloved. During the

Revolution, he was Commissary of Supplies from Pittsburgh to the Wheeling. He was Colonel for twenty-two years. His second son, Moses, born the 17th of September, 1763, was often out scouting -- Colonel of one of the Regiments of the County -- died the 29th of April, in 1832.

OTHER FRONTIER LEADERS

Colonel William Crawford had but one full brother, Valentine. He lived on Bullskin, near Charleston, Virginia, in Jefferson County, Virginia. A daughter of Valentine's married Eff. Worthington (Effie), brother of Governor Thomas Worthington. In 1774, Colonel Crawford surveyed lands on Wheeling, for Colonel D. Lefferts and others. William Crawford, a son of Valentine's, was taken with Colonel Harrison, squibbed and quartered and hung up, in 1782. Colonel Crawford's son John escaped.

Major Springer was a Lieutenant at Pittsburgh and Wheeling during the Revolution.

Colonel Silas Hedges was a cousin of Colonel David Shepherd, and lived near West Liberty, and probably died there.

Colonel William Crawford was about five foot ten inches, blue eyes, fair skin, and a handsome man of middle size. Hugh Cameron, who was killed in 1782, wore a black wool hat, band with white linen. This hat was found by Williamson's men at the Moravian Towns, and some other articles identified as Cameron's.

Neither Colonel D. Shepherd nor Captain Boggs went out with Dunmore in 1774. Colonel D. Shepherd and Captain Boggs were out [in] Hand's Squaw Campaign.

Colonel David Williamson was born in 1753. He had two sisters, the older Mrs. Bass (afterward Mrs. Captain William Boggs) the eldest, born in 1749. Robert Bass was killed in

1778 on Wheeling. In 1785 Mrs. Bass married Boggs. Williamson's parents, as early as 1773, moved and settled on Buffalo. One Wallace, on Raccoon, had his wife and one child killed, their clothing found at Moravian Town. It was Eleazer who was the Captain. David did much good service.

Colonel James Paul was born in Berkeley, Virginia. He early settled with his parents in Western Pennsylvania. On Crawford's Expedition, Paul Glover and party overtook them. The Whites had parlayed and were taken while Paul ran and escaped. He was much with Brady. Spied on the frontiers. He was with Harrison.

William Zane, the father of Ebenezer, was a Quaker. Captain Samuel Mason lived on Wheeling Creek, at the Narrows. In the spring of 1782, Indians stole some of his negroes, and killed Peter Stalhaker. The Indians, a little above the Narrows, were posted behind a large rock, and shot him.

Asa Zane: In the early part of the Revolution, he served some time in the Army to the eastward as a Lieutenant. He was broken for cowardice and retired to Wheeling. Likely he was not at the First Siege of Wheeling. He was a good and useful man.

IN THE 1790s

About 1792, David Jolly's family was attacked. They were residing on the hills on Wheeling. The old man was hunting cows. It was June. The Indians were hid in the rye. They shot Jolly in the forehead, then killed Mrs. Jolly, took William Jolly and a grandson, Joseph McCabe, prisoners. The latter, being weakly, they soon killed. Young Jolly was kept near some seven years.

James Boggs was killed on the 28th of January 1791, [my] brother and the same who aided, while a boy, in 1782, in the defense of Wheeling. He, together with John Williamson (brother of Colonel David Williamson), Thomas Karr, one Whittaker, Samuel Caldwell, and Thomas Richards, went to the head of Stillwater on a hunt, killed a considerable game, hung it up on a tree beyond the reach of vermints, and went and got their horses.

They camped, on their return to Camp, on the night preceeding the attack, up Stillwater, about forty miles from Wheeling. Near day the next morning, they were fired on. Boggs's thigh was broken with two bullets, and he was tomahawked. The noise did not awaken Caldwell, who was partly covered with a blanket, and it being partly yet dark, was not observed, or if so thought to be dead, and while only one Indian was in the company, busily examining one of the new rifles just obtained, the other Indians [overlooked] the fugitives.

Caldwell awoke, jumped up, and ran off. Seven overtook Williamson, and they came in together. The others escaped. Richards was all knocked down with a war club in some spice bushes, but got away. They lost their horses, rifles with their mocassins tied to them. It was cold, had been rainy, turned to snow and some little covered the ground, with a heavy hoar-frost, and frozen ground soon wore off their stockings, and they had a severe time before they reached the settlements around Wheeling.

Robert Purdy, around 1790, early in May, having got his family in a new cabin, a little above the Narrows of Wheeling, with a blanket hung up at the door, four Indians crossed the Ohio, and in crossing got their powder wet. They discovered this isolated cabin, and in the night crept into the house under the blanket, and seized Purdy in the bed. He had quite a contest with them. They finally overpowered and killed him. Mrs. Purdy was knocked down in the yard, senseless, and her kicking child killed. Her two little girls were taken prisoners. The Indians were hungry, got some cream, etc., and had occasion to use a pail, and threw out the water, which happened to be dashed upon Mrs. Purdy in the yard. This recovered her senses, but she did not dare move, till the Indians had plundered the cabin, and decamped. She then got to the nearest neighbor.

MISCELLANEOUS

Thomas Urie was killed in the fall of 1782, out hunting with Solomon Urie, Robert Payne, and George McConnell. Thomas Urie was killed in camp, as represented by Mrs. McNulty.

Captain Kirkwood's blockhouse, opposite Wheeling [Island], on the lower side of [Middle] Wheeling: John Wheeler killed, James Biggs and another wounded [Lee Sr's receipt answering, in Colonel Shepherd's papers, for date for James Biggs -- LCD]. The fort was directly on the river bank, half a mile above the mouth of Wheeling, on second bank. This fort was erected previous to 1777. The southwest corner had been partly caved away and fell, and in 1782, picketing had been placed there, so there was no bastion there.

After 1786, the old fort decayed, and a new one was erected near the mouth of Wheeling. There were several cabins on the north end and east side of the Fort -- quite a number of Rigger's.

In 1783, a young married woman, a Mrs. Walker, was captured on Buffalo Creek, taken to the head of Fish Creek, and there she escaped and returned to her distressed husband.

Appendix I:
Joseph Doddridge
on the Second and Third
Sieges of Fort Henry

Doddridge's account of the First Siege of Wheeling (1777), though omitted from his Notes on the Settlement and Indian Ways, *has been printed in R.G. Thwaites and L.P. Kellogg,* Frontier Defense on the Upper Ohio 1777-1778 *(Madison 1912), pages 54-58, under the somewhat misleading title "Reminiscences of Dr. Joseph Doddridge." Misleading because he was not at the siege and was only eight years old at the time. This was almost certainly a portion of his* Notes *that he decided not to publish "for want of a correct account of these occurrences" (*Notes*, 1912 ed., p. 8), and because "Noah Zane, Esq., has professed a determination to give the public the biography of his father, Col. Ebenezer Zane" (ibid.) -- which, to be sure, he never did. The brief MS accounts of the second and third sieges follow here, from Draper 6NN:127-29.*

O N THE SEVENTH or eighth of September, 1781, the second attack on Fort Henry took place. The party of Indians was but small, consisting of eighty men. They were commanded by Pekillon, a Delaware chief. Pekillon had for a long time been considered as a friendly chief, and under that character had been spared and liberated at the capture of Coshocton by Colonel Brodhead, when all who bore the character of warriors were put to death. The amount of mischief done in this attack was but small. One lad was killed, another taken prisoner, and a George Reiger was shot through the wrist. A number of cattle, as usual on such occasions, were shot by the Indians, who, where they could not conquer, did all they could to impoverish their enemies.

On leaving Fort Henry, the party of Indians went up Wheeling Creek, and took Link's blockhouse. In this affair three men were killed, and four taken prisoners. Three of these prisoners were tomahawked the next day. On the succeeding night, a Mr. Miller, the survivor, made his escape.

The fact of this party of savages having been commanded by Pekillon served amongst other considerations to exasperate the minds of our people against the Moravians, as Pekillon was well known to many of our leading men as a chief of that part of the Delaware nation which expressed a determination to maintain peace with the United States, but very unfortunately most of the country people regarded him as a Moravian, although he was by no means a member of that party.

On the 11th day of September, 1782, a last, and indeed a very formidable attack, was made on Fort Henry, by about three hundred chosen warriors and a company of English from Detroit.

On the morning of the day of the attack, the trail of the Indians on the western side of the river was discovered by one of our men, who hastened to the fort to give the notice of the approach of the Indians. The alarm gun was fired and the drum beat, in time for the families on the Island to get into the fort, before the arrival of the Indians. At the sound of the drum, it is said, an Indian Chief exclaimed, "It is all over. We are discovered. We shall not take the fort."

At the first attack on Fort Henry, our people saw profit of making a cannon of wood. It however bursted at the first trial, without throwing the ball any distance. This afforded some diversion to the Indians. Before the last attack, a swivel carrying six-pound shots had been obtained from Fort Pitt.

Of this the Indians had no knowledge. On their march to the fort they told the Captain Pratt, who commanded the vanguard, that there was no cannon but wooden ones at Fort Henry.

About 5 o'clock, the flag staff, bearing the English colours, was planted about four hundred yards from the fort. At this, a shot from the swivel was instantly fired. As soon as Captain Pratt heard the report of the swivel and saw the effect of the ball which struck the ground near the colours, he reproached the Indian chiefs by saying "You told me that they had nothing but wooden cannon in Fort Henry. You told me a lie. That is as true a piece of metal as ever I heard, and I am used to cannon. We shall never take that fort. They will fire on us like furies." '

During the day the enemy kept out of reach of the shot from the fort, but soon after it became dark, they approached close to the stockade with an Indian's yelling and a furious fire of rifles and muskets. This was repeated several times in the course of the night. In some instances the Indians threw stones over the pickets into the fort. These were sent back to them by the garrison.

During the next day, the enemy continued the investment of the fort; but with little firing except at cattle and horses. On the succeeding night, they approached and fired at the fort as they had done the night before and indeed attempted to set fire to the fort by placing flax and hemp in some ravines close to the stockade. These they endeavoured to set on fire by discharging squibs of powder on them, but without effect. On the third day the enemy left the place; two hundred returned home, while one hundred of the best warriors, with a determination to make some exploit before their return, singled out, went up the country, and made the attack on Rice's Fort [Dodderidge's account of this attack is in *Notes on the Settlement and Indian Wars*, 1912, pp. 217-221]. In this project they were likewise disappointed.

Appendix II:
Hupp's History of the Attack
on Link's Blockhouse

This article appeared in The Intelligencer *(Wheeling, West Virginia), issue of September 18, 1882, reprinted from an issue of* The Intelligencer *in 1864. It is taken from the clipped copy in the Draper MSS. Though overwritten in the Victorian fashion, it represents the accumulated local knowledge tapped by its author, Dr. J.C. Hupp, a local historian of note, and a relative of one of the men at Link's Blockhouse. Lyman Draper has written as title to the piece, "Link's Blockhouse Taken September 1781."*

AT THE DAWN of a fine September morning in the year 1781, Captain Miller, Frank Hupp, and Jacob Fisher, set out from Miller's block house on Buffalo creek, with the double purpose of performing the dangerous duties of spies and looking for stray horses. Each had with him his trusty rifle and equipments, well supplied with powder and ball. With alert and vigorous steps they pursued a westerly course, which soon led them beyond the reach of the most distant view of their houses and into the nearby unbroken forest lying between "the three ridges" and the Ohio.

Having spent the day in unsuccessful search and scouting, returning they were overtaken by nightfall near the cabin of Jonathan Link, on Middle Wheeling Creek. Here they turned in and were greeted with the hearty kind of welcome peculiar to backwoodsmen. They were cordially invited to share the comforts of his fireside for the night, which was cheerfully accepted. What, in these perilous times, were the subjects of conversation during the evening, needs no exercise of fancy to conjecture.

Having made their supper on Indian Johnny-cake and water, with some "jerked venison" which happened to be in the cabin, they retired to their beds on the loft. It was a bright starlight night, and all nature seemed propitious for security and repose, and had it not been for the fierce barking of their dogs, no danger would have been apprehended. The men conjectured that the disturbance kept up by the dogs augured more than merely the proximity of wolves, or the hooting of owls which could be heard occasionally in different parts of the deep woods that surrounded the cabin.

Link, in his over-anxiety to render his guests contented in the enjoyment of his hospitality, insisted indifference, hoping to allay their apprehension of danger. But notwithstanding one or other of the party seemed to deploy his time alternately in disturbed rest and then with anxious solicitude for their safety, in casting watchful glances around the cabin or gazing around the opening, and on the wall-like masses of forest which loomed up dimly against the sky-light, seeming to enclose it in far stretching mountain ramparts, no visible danger could be discovered.

At length, the chirping of the wood birds and the peculiar chill and ruffling of the air which are always the precursors of approaching day, announced that the dawn was close at hand. The hooting of the owls had ceased and the dogs lay in slumber, curled down near the cabin door.

During the night a band of savages had crept cautiously and inaudibly to places of concealment near the cabin. Here they lay ambuscading the door and the path leading to the spring close by.

The men rose from their restless beds, each cheerfully acknowledging to the other that his fears of danger had been unfounded. But alas! how delusive are all human hopes and joys. Hupp and Fisher unsuspectingly opening the door, stepped down by the limpid gurgling spring, which was but a few paces below, for the purpose of performing their morning ablutions.

Immediately a discharge of rifles issued from the covert of woods and bushes nearby, killing Fisher and mortally wounding Hupp, who ran into the cabin and up on to the loft, and while exhorting his brothers not to give up, sank down into the embrace of death. The blood thirsty savages now rushed frantically into the cabin, demanding of the men to surrender immediately and hand down their guns, or they would fire the house and envelope them in flames.

In this awful crisis of trepidation and alarm, being over-powered by numbers, Miller and Link had no choice but unconditional compliance.

While their hands and arms were being firmly bound, Hupp was precipitated from the loft, dragged beyond the threshhold, and scalped.

Pickets having been detached, the first Indians of the file taking a northeasterly direction, the noiseless march commenced, leaving the mutilated remains of their victims to the mercy of wild beasts.

The prisoners, with painful anxiety for their relations and friends, now knew with certainty that the Dutch Fork settlement was doomed to speedy scalpings, captivities, and murders. A rapid march was thus continued in profound silence till they arrived at the summit of the ridge immediately east of the homestead, on land now owned by the heirs of the late Charles Rodgers, Esq. Here they were met by the returning pickets, and a halt ensued.

At this place, leaving a guard with the prisoners, the march was promptly resumed. The grand object now was to make a descent upon the cabin of Presley Peak, which strategic move was carried into successful operation, and resulted in the capture of Peak, a man by the name of Burnett, and William Hawkins.

As the relentless wretches gathered with exultant yells around the cabin, Peak essayed to make his escape through a hemp patch, in the rear of his cabin, amid a shower of bullets, which literally mowed down the hemp around him in his speedy flight. But bounding over the rude fence un-harmed by the leaden missiles, and alighting amongst the bushes that fringed the dense woods, he was intercepted and surrounded by the ubiquitous savage warriors, at that moment springing from their covert, and he was a captive.

These three prisoners having been securely bound were left in charge of a guard, when a detachment of Indians started forthwith down the creek, while another party has-tened to the cabin of William Hawkins, which was about half a mile further up the creek.

Here they captured Miss Elizabeth Hawkins. She being sick at the time prevented her making good her escape with the rest of the family, who had fled and concealed themselves in the surrounding woods.

Mrs. Hawkins lay concealed amongst the leaves and branches of a fallen tree with an infant in her arms, which she gagged well nigh to strangulation with her apron, lest its cries betray her, whilst the bloodthirsty captors of her husband and daughter passed within a few feet of where she lay, undiscovered, in agonizing terror and trepidation. And what is a remarkable fact, her little dog that followed her to her place of concealment crouched quietly quivering by her side whilst the Indians were passing.

The party going down the creek were less successful in their predatory incursion upon the cabin of Edward Gaither, which stood at the forks of the creek, near the spot where now stands the residence of John Cane, Esq. With their accustomed caution they approached the cabin in all directions with an apparent certainty of again having an opportunity of carrying into successful execution their murderous and marauding purposes. But in this instance they were foiled. At the moment of the attack on Peak and his comrades, it being less than a mile up the creek from the confluence of the streams, and in hearing of the guns, the Gaither family was about to be seated at dinner, when alarmed by the rapid firing they suddenly betook themselves to the woods near the house.

The Indians, however, did ample justice to the untouched and still smoking edibles laid on the table, which to them was an acceptable and bounteous repast. And having pillaged the house of such articles as they wished to carry along with them, set fire to it, and hastened with their plunder to the rendezvous on the ridge, where they were soon joined by the other party and its prisoners.

Some of the exultant savages gave vent to their feelings by grotesque contortions of countenance and gyrations of body. They whooped and danced and sung -- now chiming the warwhoop in concert and the fiendish yells of triumph, whilst others gave evidence of hatred and malignity of purpose, by derisive looks and by jestures [sic], by twitching of the whiskers and hair of the prisoners. Hawkins and Burnett were special sufferers from these demonstrations, the former having red hair and the latter having a superabundance of hair about his person, which characteristics are notoriously repulsive to savage taste.

These demonstrations were interpreted by the prisoners as the precursors of untold horrors yet in reservation. Contrary to savage custom as to the treatment of the generality of prisoners in such an emergency, though being faint and feeble from fright and unable to keep pace with the Indians in their hurried march, the fair Miss Hawkins was retained a prisoner and treated with the utmost indulgence and decorum. Such was her feebleness and trepidation for the moment that she fell from the horse on which the Indians had seated her, but with their characteristic indulgence and decorous forbearance with which "they are universally said to treat captive women," she was kindly reseated upon the animal and hurried forward far in the advance of the other prisoners.

An Indian council was held. The scene which quickly followed and which was the consummation of the purposes of the council was sufficient to chill the heart's blood of even savage barbarity.

The five prisoners, firmly bound, sat side by side on a fallen tree. They were approached from the rear by five large and powerful Indians, each with uplifted tomahawk in hand. Three of whom dealt simultaneous blows, and Hawkins, Peak, and Burnet lay with cloven skulls, weltering in their life's blood. The other two savages seemed to recoil from the work of atrocity that had been assigned them. But each stood with uplifted tomahawk over the head of his intended victim. In this awful moment of suspense, Miller and Link, fortunately for themselves, gave no evidence of terror or trepidation. At that moment a warbling songster of the wood struck up its mournful song from the pendant branches of an ancient monarch of the forest, overhanging the scene of this awful tragedy.

The two intended executioners immediately cowering back from their intrepid and indomitably courageous prisoners, quickly returned their tomahawks to their belts. And the whole of the savages, palpably overwhelmed with consternation and dismay, hastened to form into line with the front Indians of the file facing toward the Ohio. Miller and Link, led by long strips of rawhide had a place assigned to them about the middle of the file

Thus, with light, silent, and cat-like tread, they advanced on their retreat rapidly till they reached the banks of the Big Wheeling Creek, when, nightfall coming on, a halt was made,

a fire was kindled some distance away from the place selected for an encampment, which was quickly extinguished as
soon as it had served the purpose of cooking their scanty
evening meal.

Here, for the first time since a few moments before the
enactment of the tragic scenes first related, was Miss Hawkins cheered with the sight of any other prisoners. With
strong filial affection she strained her eyes in anxious search
along the approaching file for a sight of her father. But when
she saw only Miller and Link, she immediately divined what
had happened.

Becoming more composed, reason and judgment were
measurably under her control, and her familiarity with the
Indian character and peculiarities admonished her that she
should not betray to the keen perceptions of the redskins the
real state of her feelings. With a resolute endurance and a
heroism befitting the occasion, she succeeded in stifling the
better feelings of her nature. And affecting indifference to
what had transpired within the last few hours, she partook,
with apparent cheerfulness, of the parsimonious and frugal
entertainment, which the Indians served up to her and the
other prisoners.

From the indistinguishable jabbering among the Indians,
it was evident they were arranging to get that sleep of which
they had so long been deprived, and to make a judicious and
safe disposition of the prisoners for the night. At length they
stretched themselves out upon the ground with such an
arrangement that on either side of each prisoner was an
Indian. As a further precaution to security, the end of the
thong by which each prisoner had been led in the march, was
securely fastened around the body of an Indian. Doubly
bound as they were, the prisoners gave up all hope of escape.

The Indians soon fell asleep. Their minds were too busy,
their nerves too excited, and the torture from their bonds too
intense, to allow the prisoners any inclination to close their

eyes. Pinioned and didtributed as they were amongst the savages, they were precluded the possibility of any communication with one another by word or even jesture.

Miller, notwithstanding his anxiety of mind and distress of body, had matured a plan for his escape. Which was to sunder, by means of his teeth, the tough thongs which served to bind him so securely. He impatiently waited for midnight, when the sleep of the Indians would be most likely to be profound.

Time passed away, and at last even Link and Miss Hawkins sank into a fitful slumber. Miller, imploring divine aid, embraced this as the auspicious moment to begin the difficult and dangerous work he had in contemplation. With an unconquerable will and unfaltering determination, he labored arduously for some time, accomplishing but little.

Though having a set of good teeth, he at times almost despaired of success on account of the toughness of the material on which he was operating. But at length one of the sundered fetters dropped slowly from its deep track, where it had become embedded in the muscles of his arm.

One of the Indians turned in his sleep! Miller lay in the semblance of sleep. Ten minutes elapsed, and no further movement being observed, he resumed his effort to unfetter himself. At length his success was complete. He stole forth cautiously from the circle of his captors. Guided by the stars he was soon on the direct route back to Buffalo [Creek], where he arrived about the break of day. As soon as he entered the blockhouse alone and with his gun, the inmates divined that some awful calamity had befallen himself and his companions. When inquired of as to Hupp and Fisher, the great deep of his manly soul was broken up, and the awfully harrowing scenes of the last twenty-four hours rushing through his mind rendered him speechless. And he could only respond by pointing to the deep and purple thong-furrows in his arms, and amid the emotional throbbings of his heart and the heaving of his herculean chest, burst into a flood of unbidden tears. The abundant tribute of tears from those around him, convinced Miller that sympathy is natural in the human heart.

The sad events of the day previous having been learned, it was desirable to extend the rites of sepulchre to those who had fallen. Among those who shouldered their rifles and set out, headed by Captain Miller, to perform these last sad rites, were John Miller, Andrew Deeds and Jacob Deeds, and Jacob Rowe.

Even after the lapse of many years, Captain Miller could seldom be induced to recount these tragic scenes in which he acted so conspicuous a part, so indelibly impressed upon his sensitive soul were their thrilling reality, and so harrowingly painful to him were their rehearsal. And when through feelings of friendship he was constrained to narrate them, it was with tears streaming down his manly cheeks.

Notes [by J.C. Hupp] (To the Original Text, 1864)

About three miles south of West Alexander, Pa., and on the right bank of Middle Wheeling Creek, and on the land now owned by Robert Erskine, Esq., was the site of Link's cabin. We were recently piloted by S. M. Bell, Esq., and the venerable William Porter, Sr., to the spot where, eighty three years ago, this rude cabin stood. Traces of its ruins are still to be seen. It stood only a few feet from the West Virginia line.

Hawkins's cabin stood a few feet south of where the National Road is now located, within easy view of Vienna, on the Hempfield road, and near the foot of what is known as "Hawkins Hill," on land owned by John Conner, Esq. The stable on the north side of the road here was constructed of the logs from this ancient cabin.

This infant was William Hawkins, who was County Surveyor of Washington county, Pa., about the year 1820.

Link was not so successful as Miller in his endeavors to escape. He was dragged along with the Indians to their villages beyond the Ohio. And tradition says that some two weeks after his capture, he was brought back into the neighborhood and taken upon the hill back of his own cabin and in full view of it, when he was set up as a target and shot by the Indians. His remains were interred by the side of those of Hupp and Fisher, about midway between his cabin and the creek. The cut through the county road has disturbed the sepulchre of these pioneer martyrs. Here at the roadside the venerable William Porter, Sr., has frequently picked portions of human bones out of the crumbling bank.

Miss Hawkins was carried by her captors to their haunts in the interior of Ohio. Here she was led in triumph to the wigwam and with due form and ceremony adopted into the tribe. She soon learned to reciprocate that disinterested tenderness with which she was so affectionately loved by the mother of her adoption. Many years after she had been wedded to a Shawnee Chief, she returned to the neighborhood on a visit to her pale-faced relatives. But the dull monotony of civilized life having lost all charms for her, she soon returned to her wild Indian home.

The "old gun" and remnants of the equipments carried by Jacob Rowe on this occasion are now in the possession of the writer of this narrative.

Appendix III:
J.C. Hupp's Account of the Attack on Miller's Blockhouse

This article also is from The Intelligencer *(Wheeling, West Virginia) and from the pen of Dr. J.C. Hupp. Lyman Draper has given it the title "Attack on Miller's Block House, April 1782" and preserved the clipping among his papers. It appears in* The Intelligencer *for September 14, 1782, under the title "A Propos to the Fair and the Centennial of Fort Henry -- Local Traditional Reminiscences of Pioneer Life in the Region" and with the note that it originally appeared in* The Intelligencer *of November 24, 1864. It is printed here as a kind of sequel to Dr. Hupp's account of the Link's Blockhouse affair, which took place in the same area and also involved Jacob Miller. West Alexander, mentioned in the opening paragraphs of Dr. Hupp's account, is preserved today much as it was in his time, just inside the Pennsylvania border from West Virginia, just off I-70 and on the National Road (Route 40).*

IN THE SPRING of 1782 Indian hostilities commenced much earlier than usual along the western frontier. As early as the month of March hordes of savages were ascertained to have crossed the Ohio and were making their way into the settlements.

The settlers thus threatened with the massacres, plunderings, burnings and captivities, with which they had already become too familiar, were filled with spirit-stirring excitement, commingled with alarm. In this predicament of apprehension and danger, the settlers along the Buffalo valley betook themselves, with their families, to the forts and block-houses.

About three miles northeast of West Alexander, Washington county, Pa., on the right bank of the "Dutch Fork" of Buffalo, is a peninsula formed by the meandering creek on the one side and Miller's run on the other. The isthmus next to the run is skirted by a narrow strip of bottom land which expands to many acres towards the creek and its confluence with the run. The side of the isthmus washed by the creek has a bold and precipitous bluff. On this isthmus was located Miller's block-house, which was besieged by a party of about seventy Shawnees on Easter Sunday, 1782.

With their characteristic cunning and caution, the Indians arrived in the vicinity the night previous, distributing themselves in ambush around the block-house and along the paths leading thereto. Thus lying concealed among the bushes or "pea vines," behind trees or fallen timber, they awaited the operation of circumstances.

Nearly all of the men were absent from the block-house on this occasion; some of them being at Rice's Fort, which was about two miles further down the creek. Of this fact the Indians most likely were apprised, and on this account the attack on the block-house is supposed to have been deferred and the ambush protracted, in order to destroy the men on their return hither.

Of those who were in this rude shelter on that fatal Sabbath morning were John Hupp's wife and four children, Mary, Margaret, John, and Elizabeth, Jacob Miller and several of his family, the family of Edward Gaither, and an old man named Matthias Ault.

The devotional morning appeal had ascended with its wonted fervor to the Father of Mercies for preservation and protection. The sun had appeared above the eastern hill tinging with its feeble rays the summits of the lofty trees of the dense forest that surrounded this primitive place of defense. The quietude of the woods was undisturbed save by the occasional chirp of the wooded songster carolling his morning anthem.

One of the matrons of the block-house had fearful forebodings that some terrible calamity was about to befall her husband, and followed him to the door, entreating him not to carry into execution his determination to accompany his friend on that morning in search of a colt that had strayed. The night previous she had dreamed that a "copper snake" struck, fastening its fangs into the palm of her husband's hand, and that all her efforts to detach the venomous reptile were unavailing -- this vision she interpreted as ominous of evil to her husband. But notwithstanding the entreaties and importunities of his wife, John Hupp set out in company with his friend Jacob Miller in search of the estray.

They entered the path leading across the run and through the woods in a northeasterly direction, and were soon out of view.

Soon the quietude of the woods was disturbed by the crack of a rifle, quickly followed by a savage war whoop issuing from that portion of the forest into which Hupp and Miller had entered. This alarm filled the minds of the women with consternation and apprehensions as to their fate. But Hupp being in the prime and vigor of manhood, fleet and athletic, if merely overpowered by numbers, his prompt return to the block-house was confidently expected. But he had fallen a victim to the foe that lay concealed, patiently awaiting the approach of some ill-fated person.

The two unsuspecting men were allowed to follow the ambushed path unmolested till they reached the second little ravine on land now owned by William Miller, Esq. Here from this concealment behind fallen timber, a savage fired upon Hupp, wounding him mortally; he, however, after he was shot, ran sixty or seventy yards and sank to rise no more.

Miller, being an elderly man, was boldly rushed upon by the murderous wretches with loud and exultant yells, and tomahawked on the spot.

Flushed with success, the savages now left their hapless victims scalped and pilfered of all clothing, to join in the beleaguering of the block-house.

While this tragic scene was being enacted, the wild excitement and confusion amongst the women and children in the block-house, with no male defender but the old man Ault, can be more readily imagined than described.

But at this trying moment Providence panoplied a female hero with courage sufficiently unfaltering for the dire emergency in the person of Mrs. Ann Hupp. Having now realized the dread forebodings of her vision, and shaking off the shackles of despondency, she turned to calm the moral whirlwind that was raging amongst the frantic women and children -- to inspire them with hope and to rally the only and infirm male defender.

She in the meantime had deputed Frederick Miller, an active lad aged about eleven years, as messenger to Rice's Fort for aid. But in this strategy she was foiled. For the lad had gone willingly and heroically only a few hundred yards down the peninsula on his dangerous embassy when he was intercepted by the Indians. Retracing his steps, he was pursued by two ferocious Indians with hideous yells and uplifted tomahawks.

This frightful race for life was witnessed from the block-house with anxiety the most intense. Every moment it seemed as though the lad would fall with cloven skull beneath the deadly stroke of one or the other of the two blood-thirsty pursuers, each vieing with the other which should strike the fatal blow. A fence had to be scaled by the boy without a blunder, or death -- certain instant death -- was his doom. Summoning all his boyhood and failing strength, he leaped the barrier, touching it merely with his hand as the foremost Indian's tomahawk struck the rail, accompanied by a yell of disappointment, when both Indians fired at him. One of the balls took effect and passed through his flexed arm, shattering the bones both above the elbow and between the joint and the wrist, whirling the lad around several times. Now subdued shrieks of terror commingled with joy were heard in the block-house as the female hero who sent out the boy ambassador received him in her arms as he bounded to the door, exhausted from the race and the loss of blood.

At this moment the Indians, leaping from their concealment, appeared in every direction around the block-house, and a hot and continuous firing was commenced. The female band, with the now trembling and weeping Ault as their counsellor, in despair and anguish were forced to the conclusion that the blockhouse would soon be taken by storm or envelope them in its flames, and with no hope of a successful resistance were about to "give up." Again, in the crisis of terrible trial and danger, Mrs. Ann Hupp proved equal to the emergency. Encouraging the trembling Ault and the weeping women with the consoling language of hope -- nerving her arm and steeling her heart to the severe duties of the moment, she, with true Spartanism, snatching up a rifle, fired at the approaching Indians, and then "ran from port hole to port hole," protruding its muzzle in different directions -- to convey the idea of great forces in the house -- at each presentation causing Indians to cower behind trees or other objects for protection.

This happily conceived and promptly executed strategy of the pioneer heroine, without doubt, saved the handful of women and children from what otherwise was inevitable -- a wholesale massacre.

A party of the Indians had taken shelter behind a stable that stood not far from the block-house. Emboldened by their firing not being promptly returned, one of them would occasionally step out to view, holding up before himself, as a shield, a clapboard, and then quickly retreat again to his shelter. At length he stepped out boldly into an open space, defiantly stretching his savage frame high in air, at which Ault was prevailed upon to fire, but palpably without doing any harm. This exasperated the besieging foe, causing the assault to become still more terrible.

At this state of the siege, the women saw and recognized three of their men approaching in great haste from the direction of Rice's Fort, when they commenced screaming at the top of their voices and beckoning the men in the direction they supposed to be the safest point to pass the Indians in gaining the block-house.

While the Indians stood in confusion and wonderment, not comprehending the meaning of the screams, the men rushed forward, passing very near to where some of the savages stood, and before the Indians sufficiently recovered from their surprise to fire upon them, they, faces red and turgid from race, bounded into the block-house unscathed.

The names of these three daring spirits, who thus perilled their lives to save their helpless mothers, brothers, and sisters from savage fury, or perish with them, were Jacob Rowe, Capt. John Jacob Miller, and Philip Hupp.

After the arrival of these men, the boldness and fury of the Indians abated, and during the remainder of the day only occasional shots were exchanged. Evidently filled with chagrin and disappointment, they skulked about the neighborhood till nightfall, and nothing more was heard of them. They, no doubt fearing a reinforcement, left during the night, bearing away with them only the scalps of Hupp and Miller.

The loss to the neighborhood of these two men was severely felt at a time when men were so much needed; but all hearts in that block-house were overflowing with thanks and gratitude to a kind and merciful Preserver for vouchsafing to them his aid and protection when their great and terror-fill-

ing peril was impending and for saving them from the ruth-
less hands of the merciless savages.

About noon on Monday, the men ventured out from the
block-house, going sadly and cautiously in search of Hupp
and Miller, with the purpose of performing for them the last
sad rites of the dear departed. They found the body of Miller
lying near the bloody path, and following the traces of blood
on the leaves and other objects over which Hupp had run,
after he received the mortal wound, his remains were promptly recovered.

Their mutilated and frozen bodies were borne to the
peninsula and laid side by side a few yards from the block-
house in the same grave, with "puncheons" for their coffin;
and today lying clustered about the graves of these two
pioneer martyrs [are] the remains of Jacob Rowe, Capt. John
Jacob Miller, Frederick Miller, the heroine Mrs. Ann Hupp,
and her daughter, Mrs. Margaret Titus. When living, the
cement and panoply of affection and good will bound them
together at once in the tender, natal, social, and moral ties of
domestic kindness, friendship, and love, and the union for
defence, and when dead they were not separated.

Notes [by J.C. Hupp] (From the Original Text, 1864)

*Miller's Block-house stood on land now owned by
William Miller, Esq., about midway between his residence at the "Old Graveyard." Here, too, is the perpet-
ual spring now in use by the fourth Miller generation,
from which eighty-two years ago this beleaguered
block-house received its supply of water.*

*After the loss of her husband, Mrs. Hupp and her
children, in accordance with her own wish, were taken
by her brother-in-law to his cabin on the bank of the
Monongahela, near where the village of Millsborough
now stands, where they remained about four years
and returned to Buffalo [Creek], where she contracted a*

second marriage with John May, and subsequently Benjamin, Ann, and George were added to the family, as before enumerated. She died on the 2nd day of June 1823, in the 66th year of her age. Two of her children, George May and Mrs. Elizabeth Rodgers, still survive, the former residing in Nebraska Territory -- the latter on Buffalo Creek, who having seen the pioneer heroes and heroines of their youth one by one gathered to their fathers, they now stand the last of a race who learned from their lips these thrilling incidents of pioneer life.

Jacob Rowe, being about ten years old in the fall of 1776, when in company with his mother and three brothers and his father, Adam Rowe, on their way to Kentucky, made a hairbreadth escape from the Indians at a point not far from the mouth of Grave Creek. Here the little caravan was attacked by a party of marauding savages who killed Mrs. Rowe and her eldest son and captured Daniel, the youngest son. Jacob escaped by running into a thicket of willows near at hand when closely pursued by a large muscular Indian, who had his little brother Daniel a captive on his back -- and this is the last account ever heard of the captive boy.

After his escape, Jacob, trembling with fear, traveled all the day stealthily through the wild and dense woods -- along the deep and dark hollows and over the precipitous hills lying in his way back to Buffalo [Creek], and when nightfall overtook him with all its hideousness in the midst of the deep woods, he, overcome with fright, fatigue, and hunger, nestled himself down among the leaves at the root of a fallen tree for the night. (He died of a throat affection which without doubt was founded on that cold, dread, and dreary November night.) The next day he arrived at Buffalo and was received into the arms of his sister, Mrs. Ann Hupp, to whom the weeping lad related the tragic scenes he had witnessed on the previous morning.

Adamdam Rowe and his son Adam also returned to the neighborhood and afterwards emigrated to Kentucky, but Jacob remained with his sister and was her survivor some three or four years.

Frederick and Capt. John Jacob were the sons of the unfortunate Jacob Miller. Frederick died on the 27th day of March, 1814, aged 43 years, and Captain John Jacob Miller died August 20th, 1830, aged nearly sixty-eight years.

Appendix IV:
Lydia Cruger's Affidavit (1849)

This affidavit is printed in Wills DeHass, History and Indian Wars of Western Virginia *(Wheeling 1851), pp. 280-281.*

THE UNDERSIGNED, HAVING been applied to for a statement of facts respecting the memorable achievement at the attack on Fort Henry, (Wheeling,) in September 1782, known as the "Gunpowder exploit," would state as follows, viz:

On Monday afternoon, September 11, 1782, a body of about 300 Indians, and 50 British soldiers, composing part of a company known as the Queen's Rangers, appeared in front of the fort, and demanded a surrender. These forces were commanded respectively by the white renegade Girty, and a Captain Pratt.

The demand for a surrender was of course uncomplied with, and the attack then commenced.

During the forenoon of Tuesday, September 12th, the enemy having temporarily withdrawn from the attack, but occupying a position within gunshot of the fort, those within the stockade observed a female leave the residence of Colonel Zane, and advance with rapid movements towards the fort. She made for the southern gate, as it was less exposed to the fire of the enemy. The gate was opened immediately, and she entered in safety. That person was none other than Molly Scott, and the object of her mission, was to procure powder for those who defended the dwelling of Colonel Zane. The undersigned was at that time in her 17th year, and remembers with perfect distinctness every circumstance connected with the incident. She saw Molly Scott enter the fort, assisted her in getting the powder, and saw her leave, and avers most positively that she, and she alone, accomplished the feat referred to, and deserves all the credit there may be attached to it.

The ammunition at that time was kept in the "store-house," adjoining the residence of my father, known as the "Captain's house." My father having left for help on the commencement of the attack, and I being the oldest child under the paternal roof, was directed by my mother to go with the messenger (Molly Scott), to the store-house, and give her whatever ammunition she needed. This the undersigned did, and will now state without the fear of contradiction, that the powder was given to Molly Scott, and not to Elizabeth Zane.

The undersigned assisted said Molly Scott in placing the powder in her apron, and to this she is willing to be qualified at any time . . .

Elizabeth Zane, for whom has long been claimed the credit of this heroic feat, was at that time at the residence of her father, near the present town of Washington, Pa. . . .

At the time of its occurrence, the achievement was not considered very extraordinary. Those were emphatically times when woman's heart was nerved to deeds of no ordinary kind; -- we all felt it was then "to do or die;" and the under-signed does not hesitate to say, that more than one within the little stockade at Wheeling, would have accomplished the feat with as much credit as the one whose name seems destined to an immortality in border warfare.

But undersigned does not wish to detract any from the heroism of that feat, she only desires to correct a gross error -- to give honor to whom honor is due. This she deems imperative, that the truth and justice of history may be maintained.

The undersigned disclaims all unkind feelings towards any one, in relation to this statement. Elizabeth Zane was one of her earliest acquaintances, whom she knew to be a woman brave, generous and single-hearted.

Given under my hand and seal, this 28th day of November, 1849.

Lydia S. Cruger
[seal]